Beau

CW00570896

Every woman I know wants to believe that she is beautiful. Yet because of the way our culture defines beauty, many of us have a hard time really believing that this is true. Beth Redman, in her gentle and understanding style, points us toward seeing ourselves through our Father's eyes. She encourages us, in very practical and real ways, to let go of thought patterns and habits that can destroy us. This book is a great one for anyone on the journey of womanhood . . . the journey of truly walking out what it is to be a daughter of the King.

HOLLY WAGNER
Speaker and Author, *GodChicks* and *Daily Steps for GodChicks*

I love how Beth is disarmingly honest about her own struggles and speaks from a place of personal knowledge that God can give each of us full lives, regardless of our past or present situations. She is also extremely passionate that women are set free to be all that God wants them to be, and I believe that *Beautiful* will go a long way in helping women accomplish this. It's packed with wisdom, insight, biblical teaching, helpful tips and interesting stories—a vital read for any aspiring woman of God!

MIKE PILAVACHI
Founder, Soul Survivor
Pastor, Soul Survivor Watford
Author, *For the Audience of One* and *Soul Survivor*

Beth has a unique and natural way of communicating with young Christian women. *Beautiful* addresses pertinent issues and offers invaluable wisdom through Beth's humorous, honest and gracious style.

TIM HUGHES
Worship Leader and Songwriter
Author, *Here I Am to Worship*

I share Beth's passion to help young women grow into all that God has for them. I frequently find when I am speaking that women nationwide are feeling frustrated and that they are failing. *Beautiful* is an easy-to-read book with simple biblical applications that will lift women from the bondage of worldly expectations to living beautifully in Christ—wholly expectant! Let Beth help you be truly beautiful!

MARITA LITTAUER
President, CLASServices Inc.
Speaker and Author, *Wired that Way* and *You've Got What It Takes*

If I wasn't sure before that being a woman is the most fun any human can have on the planet, reading *Beautiful* confirmed it. How wonderful to be reminded that each of us is predestined, planned and wanted by a Heavenly Father who thinks each gorgeous one of us is the bee's knees.

ALY HAWKINS
Author, *Soul Sister: Shine*

Beautiful

BETH REDMAN

Regal

From Gospel Light
Ventura, California, U.S.A.

PUBLISHED BY REGAL BOOKS
FROM GOSPEL LIGHT
VENTURA, CALIFORNIA, U.S.A.
Regal **PRINTED IN THE U.S.A.**

Regal Books is a ministry of Gospel Light, a Christian publisher dedicated to serving the local church. We believe God's vision for Gospel Light is to provide church leaders with biblical, user-friendly materials that will help them evangelize, disciple and minister to children, youth and families.

It is our prayer that this Regal book will help you discover biblical truth for your own life and help you meet the needs of others. May God richly bless you.

For a free catalog of resources from Regal Books/Gospel Light, please call your Christian supplier or contact us at 1-800-4-GOSPEL *or* www.regalbooks.com.

This edition issued by special arrangement with Hodder and Stoughton Limited of 338 Euston Road, London NW1 3BH, England. Original title: *I Wanna Be A Woman of God!* Revised edition published by Regal Books in 2006.

Library of Congress Cataloging-in-Publication Data
Redman, Beth.
  Beautiful / Beth Redman.
    p. cm.
  Rev. ed. of: I wanna be— a woman of God!
  ISBN 0-8307-4198-4 (trade paper)
  1. Christian women—Religious life. 2. Women—Biblical teaching. 3. Women—Religious aspects—Christianity. 4. Bible. O.T. Proverbs XXXI—Criticism, interpretation, etc. 5. Redman, Beth. I. Redman, Beth. I wanna be— a woman of God! II. Title.

  BV4527.R425 2006
  248.8'43—dc22   2006002540

1   2   3   4   5   6   7   8   9   10   /   10   09   08   07   06

Rights for publishing this book in other languages are contracted by Gospel Light Worldwide, the international nonprofit ministry of Gospel Light. Gospel Light Worldwide also provides publishing and technical assistance to international publishers dedicated to producing Sunday School and Vacation Bible School curricula and books in the languages of the world. For additional information, visit www.gospellightworldwide.org; write to Gospel Light Worldwide, P.O. Box 3875, Ventura, CA 93006; or send an e-mail to info@gospellightworldwide.org.

Dedication

This book is dedicated to three amazing women of God—
Darlene Zschech, Nancy Alcorn and Wendy Virgo—whose lives
have spurred me on more than they'll ever know.

Darlene Zschech and Nancy Alcorn both pursue Jesus
with a passion and live to glorify Him day by day through their
work at Hillsong and Mercy Ministries.

Wendy Virgo, whose books inspired and blessed me as a young girl,
came into my life to mentor and encourage me at a crucial time.

Thank you to you all!

Contents

Foreword 8
Mary Pytches

Acknowledgments 10

Chapter 1 13
I Want to Be a Beautiful Woman of God

Chapter 2 17
I Want to Know I'm Wanted

Chapter 3 23
I Want to Be an Uncomplicated Woman

Chapter 4 39
I Want to Know Who I Am

Chapter 5 49
I Want to Be Like Her—Part 1

Chapter 6 57
I Want to Be Like Her—Part 2

Chapter 7 63
I Want to Be Like Her—Part 3

Chapter 8 69
I Want to Break the Cycle

Chapter 9 . . . . **93**
I Want to Have a "Big Life"!

Chapter 10 . . . . **105**
Christ in You, the Hope of Glory

Mercy Ministries of America **111**

Foreword

In traveling the world, I meet women on every continent who are unhappy and unfulfilled. They suffer from chronic low self-esteem and often confess that they hate both themselves and the way they look. And Christian women are not exempt from the insecurity that pervades our society. Much of the blame lies with our culture's overemphasis on looks. Image seems to be everything. We are bombarded with advertisements cajoling us to buy cosmetics and clothes and go on sun-drenched holidays—all of which will enhance our image and make us happy. Constantly the media parade beautifully tanned and leggy women before our eyes, making most of us feel totally inadequate—and even downright ugly.

Needless to say, the image-makers are making billions out of our obsession with our looks: liposuction, nose jobs and breast implants/reductions are all on the increase, and many women go through untold suffering just to feel good about themselves: "I want to be beautiful." "I want to be thin." "I want to be tall." "I want to be happy." "I want to look like [whoever the latest icon is]." Such is the frantic cry coming from the lips of many self-conscious, self-loathing young girls. This desperate need to be beautiful is what our culture breeds in women, and it is difficult to resist the obsession with beauty.

Beth Redman points us to a better way. She is someone who understands the wavelength of today's young women. She knows what makes them tick. She has sat where they sit. She has felt their feelings and knows their struggles. From that place of understanding, she speaks the truth about our unhealthy tendencies and encourages us to resolve the past. She shows how, with the help of the Holy Spirit, those addictive patterns can be changed, and she points us to a better way—a higher goal: to become a beautiful woman of God.

With the help of personal testimonies and an excellent chapter on breaking the addictive cycles to which we are so prone, Beth gives many helpful pointers on how we can become like the woman of Proverbs 31. There we see an uncomplicated, brave, disciplined, gracious woman whose life appears so full and worthwhile—a woman who has won the admiration of generations of women who long to develop just some of her attributes.

Beth presents all of us with a goal worth striving for—to become part of a generation of women who recognize their complete weakness, but realize God's complete strength. Women who pursue a godly life, along with faith, love, perseverance and gentleness. Women who fight the good fight and yet remain wholesomely feminine. A generation of women who live by the Spirit and keep in step with the Spirit.

This is a book that will particularly appeal to young women who are starting out on the journey of life and finding out who they are in God. But it will also greatly inspire those who have been on that road of discovery for some time but who find themselves in need of some encouragement and inspiration. I hope readers will enjoy Beth's words of wisdom as much as I have.

—Mary Pytches

Acknowledgments

My overwhelming thanks go out to:

My incredible husband, Matt—I love you absolutely and appreciate what a truly humble, faithful man of God you are.

My gorgeous children, Maisey Ella and Noah Luca—God's extravagant gift to me—and, of course, my lovely mum, Lesley.

Pete Brooks at Church of Christ the King, Brighton, England, for releasing Irene Brooks's wisdom and support every Thursday for a long time. (Irene, you are wonderful!)

Terry and Wendy Virgo at New Frontiers International; Gary and Cathy Clark at Hillsong, London; and Louie and Shelley Giglio at Passion—for their wisdom and kindness and for teaching the Bible with such power and integrity.

Everyone at our new church plant called "The Point"—these are such exciting times.

Natasha and Nikola Bedingfield, Jonas and Kiki Myrin, and Sarah, Aaron and Solomon—my "God" family.

Irene, Christy, Kimberlyn, Nancy, Sarah and Ellie, and Mary Pytches, for your invaluable contributions to the book. You are all wonderful women.

To faithful friends and sharpeners: Tim and Rach, Pete and Bee, Rach Cohn, Loretta (for always being there), Na, Anna, Miss Claire Prosser and Turid and Kier.

Finally, many thanks to the incredibly patient David Maloney and all the others at Hodder and Stoughton in London, and also to those at Regal Books in the United States.

Once again, thank you!

I Want to Be a Beautiful Woman of God

As a young girl, I was very damaged and messed up. The pain was at times unbearable —and my coping mechanisms resulted in my being an even more complicated and difficult person to be around. The grace that God showed me as I grew up in these broken circumstances was the Church. No matter what sort of desert I found myself in, God always provided the river of Church life to flow alongside me, bringing His comfort, shelter and love. I "gave my life to Jesus" about 10 times before I *actually* fully committed and surrendered my life to Him at the age of 18, when He flooded my life with His Holy Spirit.

Since that day, when I fully acknowledged who He was and grasped something of the immeasurable love and sacrifice demonstrated at the cross, I've been on a mission: to know Him more, to love Him more, to become more like Him and to make Him known to others. Even though for much of the time I was still in the same circumstances, I was not the same old me—I was a new creation. I may still have had the same reputation and labels that those in my neighborhood and church had known me by, but Jesus had cleansed me and was continuing to change me: "Though your sins are like scarlet, they shall be as white as snow" (Isa. 1:18). That was just how I felt and how I still feel today.

If ever there was a messed-up sinner in need of a hope and future, it was me. The last 10 years, though, have taught me that to press into God, being honest before Him and confessing my sin, leads to a life of wholeness and freedom. Whatever sadness, sin, suffering or crisis we may come up against, He is able to deliver, heal and restore us. The awesome God of heaven, who is surrounded by angels calling out His holy name, longs to know us and change us. Jesus—worshiped as the glorious, stunning Savior—changes lives and brings us a hopeful and glorious future. Our God brings beauty from ashes, displaying *His* beauty within us—and even transforming other people's broken lives through us. It's a mystery. It is undeserved. It is beautiful!

At the cross, our broken past dies with Jesus and our new lives rise, just as He rose. In His light, our fractured past should no longer dictate who we are or what we will become. We don't have to inherit the sin of previous generations or carry yesterday's baggage. I know who I was before I met Jesus, and I know what sort of woman I am today. And although I'm still on the journey, I've discovered time and time again that the more I cling to Him, the more He is made beautiful and glorious in my life.

So many of us women struggle with insecurity, the need to compare ourselves with others, unforgiveness, gossip, jealousy and the everyday challenges that womanhood throws at us. But when we as Christian women gather together, we have the opportunity to throw off these things and reflect Christ in a beautiful and glorious way. We don't have to live in the old. The new is beckoning.

I want to be a beautiful woman of God—an uncomplicated follower of Jesus who breaks free from the cycle of the past and lives a "big life" for God. I want to leave a legacy behind. And, through this book, I want to encourage you to do the same. May these pages draw you into God's presence and cause your spirit to cry out to Him. Let's not stay the same as we once were. He is calling us to dedicate our lives to Him, to be women of God who bring Him much glory.

Each chapter in this book is a prayer to be more like Him. The chapter titles in this book are not meant to be childish demands, but instead they are the passionate prayers of a woman desperate to take hold of the things that Christ Jesus took hold of for me. This book is my prayer, a sobering look at who I am without Him—and a glorious peek at what the future can be like because of Him.

God bless you on your journey, beautiful woman.

Love and grace through Jesus,
Beth xxx

Chapter 2

I Want to Know
I'm Wanted

On a beautiful day in Port Elizabeth, South Africa, in March 2000, the moment had finally arrived—my husband and I were going to be told the sex of our first unborn baby. The doctor squirted out the jelly and jiggled the ultrasound equipment around on my stomach and told us that the wriggling, punching munchkin inside my tummy was a girl. Intuition had told me so—a precious little girl. What an absolute blessing! We rushed to the store and bought everything in pink. We just couldn't wait to start preparing properly for our daughter's arrival.

I remember the day a friend remarked that I must be pregnant—I had left our table at the restaurant to go to the bathroom *seven* times during our meal together! As a mother of three, my friend knew all the signs.

Matt had originally thought that we should wait until we'd been married for 10 years before we had a baby, but in fact it was just two years after we were married that I became pregnant. For a long time I had dreamt of becoming a mum, but I was trying to be a good and patient wife. But then, one day God just changed Matt's heart on the matter. The next thing I knew, I was taking a pregnancy test and doing the math: I was eight weeks pregnant.

Being a sensible and practical soul, Matt decided to read the lengthy instruction booklet inside the kit before getting excited, so I was left staring at the two blue lines, overwhelmed with joy, for at least 10 minutes before Matt was convinced and joined in the celebrating! We were both elated.

Both our children were planned and wanted. From day one of conception to the time of birth, they were equally anticipated with longing and love—not just by my husband and me, but by their extended family, too. When they were both baptized, we invited the people who loved them the most to celebrate extravagantly. Our children are very blessed to be so treasured and loved by their family. That very fact is evident in the way they carry themselves through life and how they feel about themselves today.

Tragically, that is not how every infant enters the world. There are so many different heartbreaking scenarios into which millions of children are born each day—experiences and feelings that haunt and overshadow these individuals their entire lives. Perhaps they were born at the "wrong" time, are the "wrong" sex, or are from the "wrong" father. It may be that they are reminded of these facts throughout their lives. I remember one childhood friend who was told repeatedly by her dad that he had always really wanted a son. She was dressed in a soccer jersey for parties and given goalposts and gloves for Christmas.

Obviously there's nothing wrong with a girl not being "girly," and being female doesn't mean you have to be pink, clean, shiny and fluffy. There are many different expressions of womanhood.

There is, however, something very wrong with a girl disliking herself or her gender because she feels that her dad didn't get what he wanted. Sadly, in some cultures boys are considered a better, more valued commodity: a sign of good fortune and reward for their families. I read a recent statistic that claimed more than 60 percent of women have at one time or another wished they had been born men instead of women. In many places around the world today to have a son is still regarded as an honor, but to have a daughter is seen as a misfortune. But these are certainly not the thoughts of our Creator God. God wants sons *and* daughters.

> *In many places around the world to have a son is still regarded as an honor, but to have a daughter is seen as a misfortune.*

As we rejoiced and gave thanks on that day we discovered we were expecting a girl, something even more beautiful and powerful was occurring. God was rejoicing over *His* daughter—the daughter He had known about and anticipated since the beginning of time. Of course, this extravagant declaration of love clashes with the sterile and basic facts that we read about in some biology textbooks: bland text telling us we are nothing more than the coincidental result of a man's sperm fertilizing the egg of a woman.

A conception may be planned and wanted through lovemaking, or it can result from an encounter with a stranger, a miscalculation, an encounter between two people whose names are never known to the child, a horrific rape, or an incredible medical procedure in a laboratory. Whatever the emotional circumstances, as Christians, we realize that our conception is not a mere biological moment—but the unchanging biblical revelation that all of us are, in God's eyes, *predestined, planned* and *wanted.*

> Can a mother forget the infant at her breast,
>   walk away from the baby she bore?
> But even if mothers forget,
>   I'd never forget you—never.
> Look, I've written your names on the backs of my hands
> (Isa. 49:15-18, *THE MESSAGE*).

What about our gender, then? Can that be an accident? Textbooks tell us it is always the male sperm that determines the sex of the baby; a female egg only carries an XX chromosome, whereas a man's sperm carries either an XY chromosome, which results in a boy, or an XX chromosome, which produces a girl. Biologically, it appears to depend on the fate of the sperm—but that, of course, is only if you leave our amazing Creator God out of the equation. As Christians, we do not simply rely on what we know from science, but rather on what we know from the Creator of science, our Father God. In the Bible, God told various people the sex of their baby, even before they knew they were to become parents—for instance, Abraham, Hannah, Zechariah and Mary.

So we must not underestimate how living under, and being aware of, this powerful truth can erase the pain of human circumstances and bring a whole new security and confidence to our existence through living under the banner of our Father's love. This truth is illustrated by a moving story from my friend Sarah Emmanuel:

> I was privileged to grow up in a Christian home, believing in God and having strong Christian role models around me that I could learn from.

When I was six months old my dad died; he committed suicide. Because of this I grew up feeling rejected in that he had chosen not to be part of my life. My mum later remarried and for a while I called that man "Dad," but that did not work out, as he ended up in prison. I would hear my friends talking about their dads and I'd long for this; but I would tell myself I wasn't good enough to have a dad. I was angry at God to begin with, but I saw how my older brother wasn't angry and he seemed happier. I realized that being angry with God was not making anything easier, but in fact harder—because I was holding all of the pain and rejection inside of me.

I remember the first time I encountered the Holy Spirit, at a youth weekend away. There, I wept for ages, experiencing God's love for me; a love I had never known before. I chose to let God in and began to be vulnerable with Him, and as I did this He began to heal me and take away

We are wanted and loved, and we belong to God.

the pain and anger inside me. Sometimes I would close up again and get scared of letting God deep into the pain, but in times of worship I would see and experience God, and so I kept choosing to let Him in and choosing to let Him be my Father.

God met me in times of loneliness and pain. Some days I could not bear to look at myself in the mirror; but out of those hard times He has brought good, because He has restored me.

Last year, when I got married, I walked down the aisle with my head held high, thankful for all that God has

done in my life and confident in who God has made me—
a daughter of the King!

We have a Father in heaven who was expecting us and
preparing for us. We are not unloved accidents, a parent's pos-
session, or an unwitting explosion of fate. Something much
more incredible has happened to us. We are wanted and loved,
and we belong to God.

I Want to Be an Uncomplicated Woman

Women! We're a funny bunch, aren't we?! We have the potential to hurt and scar, as well as the ability to love and soothe, and we often seem to find "doing life together" really tricky. For example, have you seen the discord that *can* result from women sharing houses, offices or going on vacation together? Have you ever heard the venom of a woman hurt by another woman? Messy and frightening!

So sisters, why can't we just master the art of caring for one another, putting on love, forgiving one another, releasing one another, being pleased for one another, or hurting for one another? Why do we so often end up judging one another, talking behind each other's backs, or letting jealousy take hold? What is it in our emotional DNA that causes some of us to struggle so much in this area?

Realistically, there will *always* be the potential for catfights, gossip, insecurity and exclusivity when we women gather together. This was demonstrated in the first few episodes of the reality

TV show *The Apprentice*. On this show, an equal number of men and women were chosen to live together and compete to become Donald Trump's new executive apprentice. It certainly made for interesting viewing. The men got their suits on. The women got their claws out. However, even though both sexes had altercations, when the men would fall out, they were still able to do business and be friends. But when the women would fall out, they could not get over it . . . *ever*! It was truly vicious.

Why do we so often end up judging one another, talking behind each other's backs, or letting jealousy take hold?

Some women become defensive, sharp and difficult—or take offense easily and become unnecessarily involved in the business of others. You may have someone like that in your life and not know how to deal with her. It may even be that as you read this, you are aware that you have some of these characteristics. But there is another kind of woman—one who is open and accountable, forgiving and free. I know which type of woman it is a pleasure to share life with, and I know which one I want to be!

Uncomplicated women make for much better friends. However, I also know what sort of woman I often so naturally am. The journey to being uncomplicated involves a great deal of putting ourselves under the microscope, facing up to our faults, and asking God for help. It's easier and less painful to judge and see clearly the sin and shortfalls of others, but Scripture says, "Search *me*, O God, . . . test *me*" (Ps. 139:23, emphasis added), not "Search my friends" or "Test my pastor's wife."

How often have churches been ruined or ministries destroyed by fallouts, disagreements and, ultimately, discord? Leaders' wives are often a fond target.

I have two American friends, Kimberlyn Hall and Christy Nockels, who have a powerful testimony of how God restored a devastated friendship and ministry for His glory. Here is Kimberlyn's story of how God took something completely broken and transformed it with His powerful grace:

Jealousy. It attempts to kill and often does—but my story is one where good triumphed over evil. Have you ever lost a good friend or even your best friend? I have. When such a close friendship dies, it is one of the most painful things; yet to have seen God breathe hope, life and forgiveness back into these shattered pieces of friendship has been one of the most beautiful events in my life.

My dear friend Christy Nockels was a precious gift from God. Our husbands (they were our boyfriends back then) had a powerful and unique ministry flowing from their hearts, leading worship together. But the more connected we all became, the more complicated ministry and friendship became. We watched the blessings of God be challenged and assailed by the enemy as my friendship with Christy suffered blow after blow: comparisons, fear of intimacy, immaturity, lack of communication, pride, and a jealousy that grew stronger and stronger. Then one day it all fell to pieces. The saddest day of our friendship for me was the day we sat down to talk things through—so much pain and misunderstanding. At the end of our conversation, we both walked away, with only the hope of distance remaining.

I was so glad to be physically apart, but God kept my heart very much connected to His desire for restoration.

Through those seven years of lost friendship, the greatest thing I learned was "bless her . . . pray blessing on her life every time you think of her, every time you relive a memory, or wonder what she's doing, or hope to see her fall flat on her face, bless her." These were words from Jan Bingaman, a wise friend of mine, and being so desperate, I took her advice. I guess I was hoping to receive the "martyr's blessing" for praying for her, right? It totally backfired, and God's unfailing love rescued me from myself and started to sow a seed of reconciliation.

God kept putting Christy and me together face-to-face at random times, or her name would pop up in other places in a way I couldn't escape. Then my heart began to crack open with the birth of our first baby. While I was pregnant, word came of Christy's having a miscarriage. My heart's response was unexpected—it broke. I wept and wept, though quietly, as I was still not ready to fully accept or reveal how I loved my friend dearly. Somehow in that moment my heart felt near to the grieving heart of God for His daughter.

It took one more life event—the near loss of another close friendship—to make me fully realize I was carrying a heavy load that was not mine to hold and that I'd struggled for so long with the weight of my own emotions yet been blinded to the feelings of my friend Christy.

I got the chance to sit down with Christy a few months later and tell her what God was showing me. Now, I must tell you the "what about me syndrome" was defiantly knocking at my door. Deep inside me lingered the need for God to validate the fact that we were both in the wrong, and I was not the only guilty party. But that is the beauty of God's gift—and I do believe forgiveness is a gift. He released me from holding her in debt. I needed to be responsible for my failings. I had peace that God would shine on the rest of it in due time.

Slowly but surely God provided space in our busy lives to get together and talk through our past. We sat in Starbucks for hours. My heart filled up with deep, sisterly love, and I found myself blessing and genuinely rejoicing in things I once had been so jealous of. Christy dispelled my fears of rejection with the sweetest words of harmony and unity, kindness and forgiveness—a humbling display of the beauty of God at work in our lives.

With forgiveness came freedom. I walk in relationships differently now. I stand next to Christy and sing with all my heart, praising God that He delivers and heals. Our God displays His glory when we rest in the mercy of a good relationship.

Christy's testimony is just as powerful:

The restored relationship between Kimberlyn and me is truly nothing short of a miracle. There were some attempts early on from both sides to try to restore what had been lost, but as Kimberlyn shared, it only resulted in more hurt and anger. Working out of our flesh, I think we both wanted to be the one to "set the record straight," but I believe that God wanted to do so much in us individually and apart from one another that He completely geographically separated us! This took seven years . . .

It was so hard to watch her carry her first child as I painfully went through losing two babies by miscarriage.

Many years before this I had sketched a drawing with some art pencils of Kimber and me. We both have long, dark hair, so in my sketch I drew one with a pregnant belly sitting in a chair with her head bowed and hair covering her face. The other was kneeling at the feet of the pregnant woman, her hair covering her face as well. I remember feeling awkward as I realized that I wasn't sure which one was me in the drawing. I knew which one I wanted to be! I wanted the pregnant belly first!

Years later, God brought that picture back into my heart when I had to "swallow" the news of Kimber's pregnancy during such a painful time in my own life. I heard that still, small voice, "I want you to learn what it means to serve her, love her and get on your knees for her." What a valuable but excruciating teaching moment from the Lord.

I know that God had our healing years purposed and planned from the start, but I can't explain the joy and freedom of our restored friendship! How grateful I am to God for Kimberlyn's obedient heart in coming to me and letting Him open a door of forgiveness to mend our friendship completely. I didn't realize until we had been restored how I had allowed the enemy to put chains on me because of the hurtful things that had been said between us. I was especially wounded in the area of worship.

Because of our restoration, God has released the chains, causing me to be free in His presence to truly worship Him! I believe much of this freedom came from Kimberlyn's pressing into places where she knew that I had been wounded by her, and allowing the Lord to undo that hurt through healing words over me. There was power in this release as she gave me her full blessing, almost a sending out as a sister in the Lord to do what I'm called to do!

I can see things in Kimberlyn now that I had never seen before. I recognize her amazing gifts and rejoice in the beauty of her creativity, and I'm challenged by her walk with God. I finally feel free to bless her and to fully ask God to increase His anointing and favor on her life. "Thanks be to God, who always leads us in his triumph in Christ, and manifests through us the sweet aroma of the knowledge of Him in every place" (2 Cor. 2:14, *NASB*).

Christy and Kimberlyn made a purposeful choice to follow God and pursue restored friendship.

Recently, I've been struck by two sets of women in the Bible: Sarai and Hagar, in the Old Testament, and Mary and Elizabeth, in the New Testament. All of us possess the potential to live as enemies, like Sarai and Hagar, who clashed, resented and devastated each other; or we can be peace-loving and a blessing, like the cousins Elizabeth and Mary, who loved God and one another and whose unity played a part in ushering in the lives and ministry of Jesus and John the Baptist.

First, let's look at Sarai's life. Sarai and her husband, Abram (later known as Abraham), were unable to have children of their own. As Genesis 12 explains, they traveled and set up camp with a team of servants: "[Abram] took his wife Sarai, his nephew Lot, all the possessions they had accumulated and the people they had acquired in Haran, and they set out for the land of Canaan" (v. 5).

Included in this group of people would have been the servants' wives and daughters—and a constant stream of infants.

Many women today opt for careers and give motherhood a miss by choice, but in Sarai's day giving birth to children was as much a part of life as eating and sleeping. Without children, Sarai would have stood out in an excruciating way. She may have felt others "kindly" whispering about her and feeling sorry for her. Sarai was excluded from motherhood not by choice but by circumstances that she agonized over.

As any woman who gives birth will testify, when a baby is born you are suddenly thrust into this exclusive and almost surreal club in which people you had nothing in common with before are now your bosom buddies (literally!). Talk is dominated by babies, sleepless nights, feeding and the latest trick your amazing baby has mastered. Perhaps this exclusive atmosphere would have surrounded Sarai. Each morning as she walked out of her tent, there would have been the swelling bellies of pregnant women, newborn bundles and mothers breast-feeding all around her. It would have been an agonizing world to have been so close to, yet not part of; it would have driven Sarai almost to despair. Was it her fault that Abram would never have an heir? It must have appeared that way. After all, God had chosen to bless all these others but not her. She took a deep breath and, out of desperation, took matters into her own hands:

> Now Sarai, Abram's wife, had borne him no children. But she had an Egyptian maidservant named Hagar; so she said to Abram, "The LORD has kept me from having children. Go, sleep with my maidservant; perhaps I can build a family through her." Abram . . . slept with Hagar, and she conceived. When she knew she was pregnant, she began to despise her mistress. Then Sarai said to Abram, "You are responsible for the wrong I am suf-

fering. I put my servant in your arms, and now that she knows she is pregnant, she despises me. May the LORD judge between you and me" (Gen. 16:1–5).

So Sarai, exasperated at never coming up with the goods herself and feeling her solution was the only way an heir would be produced, foolishly and wearily nominated Hagar's ovaries to fulfill the role. A persuasive Sarai nagged Abram into doing what she thought was right and then blamed him when it all went wrong.

At this point Sarai was displaying the wrong kind of strength. She was making decisions in an emotional state, which resulted in her exerting authority over her husband and, out of pain, acting without thinking. This caused the original plan God had for the couple to take on a dramatic, unnecessary twist. God had already made a promise to Abram that they would have children. Yet Sarai, out of her brokenness, was no longer able to believe that her husband had really heard God. She felt her suffering and humiliation had became too much, and disillusionment set in.

In our own lives, there will be times when the things we believed God had promised do not come to pass.

So she made a broken, misguided decision that only increased her pain and fueled her anger.

As soon as Hagar became pregnant, something nasty started to happen. No longer just a servant, she suddenly had power and control over Sarai. She dangled her pregnancy above Sarai's nose like a foul-smelling carrot. The two became archenemies, and Sarai complained bitterly to Abram, who said: "'Your servant is in your hands . . . Do with her whatever you think best.' Then Sarai mistreated Hagar; so she fled from her" (Gen. 16:6).

Sarai's story is heartbreaking, but one that we can learn so much from. In our own lives, there will be times when the things we believed God had promised do not seem to transpire . . . or when something we dreamed of is taken away or denied for the time being.

Not long ago, Matt and I spent a long time praying about whether or not to have a third baby. It was our dream, but we just wanted to get the timing right and, if you like, get God's permission first. During this period, we were given a word that we specifically incorporated into our prayers—and we both felt it was a confirmation that the time was right.

When the pregnancy test came back positive, we were giddy with delight. All went well for the first trimester, but then at a routine ultrasound we were distraught when we were told that our little baby's heart was no longer beating.

We were so, so broken. And, at the time of this writing, we've not been able to conceive again; I've discovered that I'll need an operation in order to do so. Right now, every time I see a pregnant woman, I have to deal with the fact that it's not me—and that I don't know if or when it will be. Sarai's experience has taught me to "not be wise in my own eyes" or think God is against me. The thing that keeps me buoyant is the truth that God is for me, God is love, and God is wise. I must not write off a situation or decide what the future will look like. God is in control, holding my tears and the days to come in His powerful hands.

In spite of overwhelming pain and disappointment, we must turn to God. Sarai came to the wrong conclusion that God had canceled her heart's desire. She said to Abram, "God has prevented me," and then tried to control events herself. This caused her life to spiral even further out of control. If we feel that we are about to make a decision out of pain, we need to meditate on God, call on Him and come to Him! Psalm 4:4 tells us to "search [our] hearts and be silent."

The women who know God best and make the wisest choices in times of great difficulty are those who meditate most on Him. In periods of confusion, the voice of Scripture and the still, small voice of the Father can encourage or challenge our hearts in an instant. When jealousy burns as we painfully watch someone else prospering, God can comfort us in our brokenness—and also help us to recognize the sin of envy. If we turn to God, repent and ask Him to help us, He is able to change our hearts and comfort us. He is the enabling, forgiving, supernatural helper. We need to meditate on Him.

Can a barren woman ever hope to smile at the news of another woman's pregnancy? Yes, yes, yes! God's grace is enough for our deepest anguish, for the prayer we feel He's never heard and for the sadness that for a while we must live with. In pain, we should not take things into our own hands. We must continue to call on Him, our Savior. We need to trust Him even though our world is caving in. At times of *breakdown*, we are often nearest to a *breakthrough*.

Sarai's story also teaches us that though we suffer legitimate pain, there is no excuse for punishing another woman or starting a battle with her. We should not allow the enemy to have a foothold or start a war. Just the other day, completely out of the blue, I was verbally attacked by another woman. I saw a face I recognized from the past and walked over to greet her warmly. What a mistake that was! She burst into a tirade of unkind and untrue accusations. Immediately, anger rose up in me. This was a character assassination, an injustice and a lie! If I had opened my mouth, I knew I would have spent the rest of my day repenting—

and further still, I knew that this was a battle I would not win. I listened. I turned. I walked away. Then I committed it to God in prayer. Even in agony and injustice, we must recognize the potential for sin.

Although Hagar was only doing what her mistress had commanded her to do, she was not peace-loving and gracious. No, she fought back. Let's be women who even in suffering and injustice can offer love, show grace, persevere—and sometimes stay silent in the face of accusations. Only the Holy Spirit can assist us in doing that, but if we are mindful and ask Him, He will help. To do this brings glory and honor to God—and breathes peace into a world of cat claws and revenge.

In contrast to Sarai and Hagar, Mary and Elizabeth show us a totally different type of relationship. They came together in faith and hope to worship. Mary had every right to feel scared and intimidated at the prospect of being chosen at such a young age to be a mother and, most likely, face gossip and ridicule. She could never explain to those judging her the child whom God had called her to carry and why. Because she was just a teenager, Mary had not spent years longing for a child; she simply awoke one day to find an angel greeting her with the news of what was to come.

In contrast, Elizabeth had grown old and had longed for a child of her own for many years. She was married to Zechariah, who was a priest and a highly respected man. For this couple and their extended families, the pregnancy was a celebration.

Mary faced uncertainty and displeasure, but she chose to believe in God and rejoice. As an older, mature relative, Elizabeth could easily have felt protective and sorry for Mary (as their circumstances were so different). But as a wise woman of God, she recognized that Mary's baby was a blessing from God and spurred Mary to praise God and feel grateful by saying:

You're so blessed among women, and the babe in your womb, also blessed! And why am I so blessed that the mother of my Lord visits me? . . . Blessed woman, who believed what God said, believed every word would come true! (Luke 1:42-45, *THE MESSAGE*).

Elizabeth helped Mary to praise God and exalt the privilege of her situation. Mary responded as follows:

I'm bursting with God-news; I'm dancing the song of my Savior God. God took one look at me, and look what happened—I'm the most fortunate woman on earth! (Luke 1:46-48, *THE MESSAGE*).

Mary and Elizabeth were an amazing combination; theirs was a friendship that glorified God and saw the privilege of their situation rather than the potential pain. They decided to look to God in praise and chose together to view this as an opportunity for great blessing. They stayed with each other for three months, no doubt spurring each other on and praising God until their babies arrived.

This beautiful friendship between cousins Elizabeth and Mary and the antagonizing breakup between Hagar and Sarai prove that a disgruntled, ungrateful heart leads to the discouragement of others while a hopeful, believing heart leads to the hope of others. You can be an example, a witness and a stunning friend even in your sorrow and stress *if* you choose to put your hope in God, not in circumstances.

I'm not trying to promote an army of shiny, happy people—unreal about pain, unable to deal with sorrow—but instead honest, hopeful people who are real about what they feel yet unshaken by knowing God's sovereignty and presence even in times of trial. It's a choice. Our coming together can be beautiful and life-giving or harmful and wounding. And it's down to you and me to decide which type of woman we are going to let God mould us into. By making a choice to live this way, we may just start to pioneer something awesome and stunning for the kingdom of God.

So we have been set a challenge that depends on our making a lot of seemingly unnatural choices—but of course, Jesus does not ask the impossible of us or set a test we must face and perfect alone. He will help us. The most helpful and important thing we need to do is begin to increase our communication with God and our reliance on the Holy Spirit. Christ is *in* us, the hope of glory.

Reading as much of the Bible as we can, making a deliberate choice to do things differently, dying to self, choosing to go to God rather than open up to another, biting our lip rather than biting back, being humble when there is a clash of personalities—these are the marks of a woman on her way to becoming uncomplicated.

Our quest to become women of God means becoming Christlike. We take off the old self and put on the new. It takes a strong, dependent and godly woman not to cave in. But unity and love between us could well be our most powerful weapon. As we model them and function under their banner, they will lead to strength, healing, power, security and freedom. Many of those things escape us while we stay in broken relationships in which discord is allowed to live and fester. God can and will forgive and remodel us. To do this we must be honest and open—but most important, we must be humble and willing to go back and say "sorry" or forgive in order to go forward.

Of course, our journey and desire to be united with each other is not going to be easy, but the more we love God, the more love we will have for one another. The more we seek Him, then the more we love and lean toward the things He loves, like unity, forgiveness, peace and wholeness. And we grow to become more and more like He is: compassionate, gracious, merciful and patient. Before long, we'll find ourselves becoming the uncomplicated women of God we so desperately want to be.

Here is a little prayer to start us off on this journey:

Dear Father God,
I am so sorry if I have ever hurt other women. I am a new cre-
ation. The old has gone, the new has come. I am sorry, Lord,
and I commit myself to being an uncomplicated woman.

Help me, Holy Spirit; empower me to live this kind of life.
Speak to me, and show me my weaknesses. I am turning away
from the woman I can so easily be, and the wounds I have
dished out and received.

With all my heart I want to be an uncomplicated woman, a
good friend and an encouragement to other women. Help me to
love the women You have put in my life and in my family.

Please let me become like Mary, and in Your grace, would You
send me a friend like Elizabeth? I want to bring You glory. I
want to be a blessing. I love You, Lord.
Amen.

I Want to Know Who I Am

I love what are often termed "strong" women, but there's a right and a wrong kind of strong. One type brings life; the other brings destruction. Over the years, I've encountered a few young women who have a passionate dream to do something for God yet carry a dangerous attitude along with this goal. Their philosophy goes something like this: "No one—especially not a man—is going to stop me." You know the sort of approach—the bitter fruit of pain and brokenness. All over the world, and even in the Church, these strong yet wounded women are rising up and fighting back—but with a less-than-wholesome edge.

The question for all of us is this: Are we working out God's calling to us humbly and with reverence, gently seeking to become who He wants us to be? Or are we aggressively fighting for freedom in ways that do not match His design?

In this chapter, we are going to journey right back to the beginning and rediscover God's original design for women. I love hearing my mum tell me all about my birth and my early years: my first moments, my first tooth, my first word and my first step. But as a Christian woman, I want to know who I am in the Creator's eyes. I want to get right back to the roots of what it means to be a woman of God.

The history of women begins in Genesis. Our Creator God spoke into being the heavens and the skies, the earth, the plants and the animals. And He saw that all of it was good. But God's intention wasn't to create this beautiful scene and then just sit back in a lawn chair admiring His handiwork. Our God is a God of relationship, and He hadn't yet finished with creating:

> Then God said, "Let us make man in our image, in our likeness, and let them rule over the fish of the sea and the birds of the air, over the livestock, over all the earth, and over all the creatures that move along the ground." So God created man in his own image, in the image of God he created him; male and female he created them (Gen. 1:26-27).

That's our history—the story of how we were made in His image, both male and female: each sex so different, yet both made in the image of the same God.

Genesis then tells us that God said, "Rule over the fish of the sea and the birds of the air and over every living creature that moves on the ground" (v. 28). It is clear that we were created to be in partnership and to rule together with men, with the combination of both male and female gifts and personalities being equal in God's eyes. Elsewhere in Genesis, we read:

> The LORD God formed the man from the dust of the ground and breathed into his nostrils the breath of life, and the man became a living being. The LORD God took

the man and put him in the Garden of Eden to work it and take care of it. The LORD God said, "It is not good for the man to be alone. I will make a helper suitable for him." Now the LORD God had formed out of the ground all the beasts of the field and all the birds of the air. He brought them to the man to see what he would name them; and whatever the man called each living creature, that was its name. So the man gave names to all the livestock, the birds of the air and all the beasts of the field. But for Adam no suitable helper was found. So the LORD God caused the man to fall into a deep sleep; and while he was sleeping, he took one of the man's ribs and closed up the place with flesh. Then the LORD God made a woman from the rib that he had taken out of the man, and he brought her to the man. The man said, "This is now bone of my bones and flesh of my flesh; she shall be called 'woman,' for she was taken out of man" (Gen. 2:7,15,18-23).

Isn't it nice to know that we weren't some kind of afterthought? It wasn't that Adam tried to go it alone but then grew lonely, leading God to later decide to make women! We were designed from the beginning for partnership.

Isn't it nice to know that we weren't some kind of afterthought?

When Adam was given the task of naming the animals, don't you think he noticed they were all in pairs? Don't you think he noticed that everything came in twos—apart from him? He may even have noticed that he had a need that had not yet been met— a need that God, of course, already knew about. In Genesis 2:18, we read, "The Lord God said, 'It is not good for the man to be alone. I will make a helper suitable for him.'"

So that's the Old Testament story of *how* women came into being. But what was God's design for our role? The passage above says our true purpose is to be a "helper." I didn't used to like the sound of that word. It reminded me of someone stuck endlessly in the kitchen doing the dishes! Yet if we study Scripture more closely, we can see that being a helper is not an insult or a description of a second-rate job, for no less than *14* times in the Bible is God *Himself* described as a helper!

In fact, to be a helper is an amazing privilege and is a calling that requires great strength of character. Yes, at times it may involve sacrificial serving and caring roles, but there is far more implied by this word than these sorts of responsibilities. To be a helper may equally involve leadership, discipling, mentoring, teaching and decision-making. So we can see that being a helper can mean a great many different roles.

The role of being a helper is not just relevant in the context of a marriage relationship. We need helpers throughout the Church and throughout the workplace. We need women coming alongside with their creativity, their intuition and their wisdom.

There are, of course, some cultures and church environments that even now view women as those who help "back out in the kitchen." A while ago, Matt and I were hosting a meeting of leaders. I brought in some coffee and cake but quickly realized I was not invited to join "the boys." The only time I was acknowledged was when the coffee had run out! My husband was really embarrassed and felt awkward that I was being treated in this way. In this day and age, it seemed really shocking.

Of course, hospitality is a great gift (and one that I am passionate about), but there is more to me, and other women, than that. I found myself wondering how these male leaders viewed me—did they think I would start crying for no reason or start talking about my period?! I found myself feeling ashamed of feeling humiliated because I was a woman, and I was saddened that I could not sit with Matt on this occasion, hearing firsthand about the exciting things God was doing. It wasn't even that I thought I *deserved* to be in the meeting—more that I was shocked to realize that even now, in my generation of the Church, women are still subject to prejudice. Sadly, there are many other women in the Church who have had this sort of experience.

Many extremely harsh things have been said about women through the ages. Plato warned that a man who lived a poor life would be reincarnated as a woman. Aristotle said, "Woman equals mutilated male." Josephus wrote, "Woman is inferior to man in every way." A Jewish man's prayer gave thanks that he was born not a Gentile, a slave or a woman; and in parts of Jewish culture, women were "things"—they had no rights at all. They were more like possessions—like pieces of furniture—than people. Even in parts of the world today, many women have no rights at all, and no choices. They cannot live under the original breath of life that says, "Go and rule together; go and be a helper."

And, sadly, in the long history of the Church, women have often suffered simply because they *are* women. Here's a quote from the first-century theologian Origen that makes me furious: "God does not stoop to look at anything that is feminine." Origen's view was that God doesn't bother with females—that He is simply not interested in them.

In complete contrast to Origen, I have often found myself imagining that in the moment when God created Eve, while Adam slept, the almighty Creator stopped for a moment in a pause of pure delight. I remember when my daughter was born.

I was overcome with delight, and in those early moments I caught her eye, and she caught mine. I just couldn't believe that this little thing lying there was my own child. My own beautiful daughter; her little toes were like my toes, and her little eyebrows were like my eyebrows.

Don't you think that's how God the Father would have looked at His precious daughter Eve that day, and every precious daughter since? Origen would have us believe that God is not interested in us—that the real occasion was the "Adam moment." But God did not delight over one sex more than the other. He delighted over both.

The extreme feminist backlash says "we don't need men" and tries to grasp back what society tells us has been taken from us. But the way of humility gives us different wisdom.

Women have these amazing origins and yet such a broken past. What does the future hold for us? The temptation might be to say "enough is enough" and rise up to reduce men in the same way that they have reduced us in the past. The extreme feminist backlash says "we don't need men" and tries to grasp back what society tells us has been taken from us. But the way of humility gives us different wisdom: God made men and women to need each other's contrasting strengths, personalities and gifts. We must celebrate our different qualities, thanking God for our male leaders and realizing that one sex cannot function at full strength without the other.

Over the years, I've been to some women's meetings and felt almost scared of some of the women there—because on the *inside* they're rather like bodybuilders. It's easy when we've been hurt to harden ourselves in order to get through life. That's the world's way, certainly, but it's not God's way. I for one don't want women to take over the world. I want to work alongside men. I want to enjoy being involved in the things that are right for me and that use my particular qualities. I don't want to be held back, but I don't want to kick my way into freedom either.

That day back in Eden, God created a woman because that's what He chose to do. He wanted us to be part of things and very involved. He loves and cherishes His daughters—He doesn't have that "favor thing" with boys that we may have observed or experienced with some earthly fathers. God has plans for us; His purpose is for us to live out our lives under the affection and affirmation of a perfect Father. That is God's design for us—we were created beautiful and whole, and free.

But for many of us, that is our main battle—to live life confidently in our physical shell, at ease with our inner selves. Lots of us fight against thinking we're not beautiful, not whole—and it leaves us in chains, robbed of the freedom to be all that God has called us to be.

Genesis 2:25 says that Adam and Eve were both naked and felt no shame. But after the Fall, the eyes of both of them were opened and they hid (see Gen. 3:7). Many of us today are rather similar—we feel insecure as we unfavorably compare our looks with those of other women and want to hide behind a tree. God certainly doesn't want us to be victims of that particular disease of women: being ashamed of our looks, shape or size, and other external things. When we feel insecure or inferior in this way, we need to *choose* to keep living in God's truth—no matter what anyone has said to us or tried to put upon us (or even those things that we may have tried to put upon ourselves). It's crucial that we focus on His truth, not that of the world.

I for one don't want to be a victim of this particular "women's disease." I don't want to be plagued by that sense of inferiority or limited by a sense of insecurity. I want to be what God has created me to be. I long to be living more like that first woman He created in Eden: whole, at peace with herself, and free from all of the discontent that plagues the hearts of so many women in this world. I don't want to spend my life wishing I were someone else and that I had someone else's body.

As Christians, we don't need to buy in to today's focus on physical beauty that encourages women to have plastic surgery to eliminate their wrinkles or change whatever it is they are not happy with. Surveys show that plastic surgery is more popular now than ever and that a staggering 80 percent of women want to change at least one part of their body—the most popular area being the stomach, followed closely by the breasts. Clearly unhappy with themselves, such women won't rest until that part is "fixed" by going under the knife.

But surgery cannot cure our insecurity: Only Christ can enter into that deep-rooted body obsession and depression and bring contentment and freedom. Instead of a life focused on our faults and the shallow earthly trophy of outward beauty and body perfection, we need to radiate the inward beauty that comes from His glory.

Of course, it is good to look after His temple by exercising and eating healthily, and of course reconstructive surgery after some sort of accident or illness is something totally different. What I am referring to here is the pursuit of physical perfection—the need to change the person we were born to be because of society's obsession with physical beauty. Those who have had plastic surgery for these reasons often say that it doesn't bring the contentment they had hoped it would. Frequently, once they start, they end up wanting to change all the other bits they don't like: ears, nose, breast enlargement or reduction, liposuction— the list is endless.

Magazines and advertisements show us beautiful faces and bodies to compare ourselves with. We sit on a beach in our swimwear, glancing enviously across the sand at the girl with the perfect figure. For most of us, it is almost impossible not to be aware of what we see as our own imperfections. How scary it is that there are so many surgeons ready to make so much money off healthy but insecure women.

In America, I heard lots of stories about fathers buying their daughters breast enlargements or nose jobs for their birthdays or graduations. This is one gift I knew my heavenly Father was not giving me permission to have (nor was my husband, by the way!). Instead, He wanted to give me the gift of peace, contentment and security in my own skin—whether it be tanned, blemished, wrinkled or perfectly line-free.

Isaiah 61 speaks of all that God longs to give us in exchange for all the *brokenness* we possess:

> [He will] bestow on them a crown of beauty instead of ashes, the oil of gladness instead of mourning, and a garment of praise instead of a spirit of despair. They will be called oaks of righteousness, a planting of the LORD for the display of his splendor (v. 3).

Whatever journey we are on and whatever identity crisis we sometimes struggle with, in Christ there is a new day and a beautiful new freedom for all women.

I Want to Be Like Her – Part 1

Sharpening Each Other

One Bible passage that has brought incredible encouragement to my life is a really simple verse from the book of Proverbs: "As iron sharpens iron, so one man sharpens another" (27:17).

The company we keep affects us and the person that *we* are impacts others. So if we want to sharpen, inspire and challenge others, we need first to *be* iron and then *find* iron. A woman who wants to become iron is simply acknowledging a desire to grow and mature in God. Iron is solid, unbendable—a force to be reckoned with.

To become strong and to have our feet on rock in times of crisis, we must first and foremost cultivate a personal relationship with Jesus and then depend on Him solely as the One who meets all needs—the true source of our security, identity and strength. We must also lean on God's Word—the Bible itself. Storing up truth will make us more like iron throughout times of trauma, times of searching, and when we need wisdom.

In the book of Titus, Paul passionately writes to the Church and encourages them to know the truth that shows how to live a godly life. In chapter 2 of Titus, Paul gives specific instructions for men and women:

> You must teach what is in accord with sound doctrine. Teach the older men to be temperate, worthy of respect, self-controlled, and sound in faith, in love and in endurance. Likewise, teach the older women to be reverent in the way they live, not to be slanderers or addicted to much wine, but to teach what is good. Then they can train the younger women to love their husbands and children, to be self-controlled and pure, to be busy at home, to be kind, and to be subject to their husbands, so that no one will malign the word of God (vv. 1-5).

That sounds so much like the woman of God I long to be—to get on top of my current stresses and grow in grace into a great wife, mum, friend, servant and teacher. Sometimes, to reach that place, not only do we need to get to know Jesus and His Word, but we younger ones, as Paul suggests in the above passage, also need the encouragement and training of older, more mature women. A modern word for that sort of relationship is "mentoring." In other words, a sharpening relationship occurs as a more mature Christian begins to spur on and disciple a younger Christian, either on a one-to-one basis or in a small group.

Finding a Mentor!

For a few years we were involved in a church with a lot of young people—which often meant that even though we were only in our mid-20s, we were some of the oldest people there! Many of us would gather to sharpen one another and be "sistas," but sometimes we desperately craved the dynamic input from the "mothers" in God: the older women who could teach, train and encourage. In many churches today that dynamic is being stirred up and implemented, but sadly it's still not quite enough. Many women that I have spoken to have longed for someone older than themselves to look to and learn from; someone to gain wisdom from and help them along the way as boyfriends, engagements, church politics and everyday trials come their way.

This is one time when we know that we women are not making high-maintenance demands. Titus 2 shows us that we *need* that mentoring relationship of training and encouragement if we are to live the godly lives we desire so much.

We need to start the cycle of mentoring, training, discipling and mothering—even in our 20s and 30s.

So what do we do if we can't find this more mature woman to help us? Well, first we must deliberately become to others what we desire for ourselves, and there is something truly selfless and beautiful about this. We need to start the cycle of mentoring, training, discipling and mothering—even in our 20s and 30s. So if there is a younger Christian woman in your world, as the older woman you need to find a way to start loving her and spurring her on.

Second, we need to pray for a mentor of our own. I prayed fervently for someone to help me out in the early days of being a mother—I just felt so overwhelmed with two babies under the age of two. An amazing woman, Wendy Virgo (whose books I had read as a young girl), happened to be in my church, and she invited me to become her prayer partner. It was such an uplifting, inspiring season, and the fruit of those times pushed me to make sure I was being that sort of blessing to younger women in my world.

On a totally different level, it's a real blessing these days that satellite television can, for those who have it, beam into your home the most amazing and godly women. Joyce Meyer, for instance, is an incredible woman of God who has a Bible study that airs on satellite television here in the United Kingdom—she also has a free monthly magazine that is truly inspiring. Many times, I have used her words to encourage some of the younger women around me.

> *We all have the most incredible mentor of all to lean on—the precious Holy Spirit, the Counselor, who breathes hope, joy and wisdom into us.*

Alternatively, there are many credible Christian conferences solely for women, and if you can get to one of these, you will be really encouraged, breathed into and inspired. While these events are, of course, not the whole picture, personally I've found that some of them have given me the most valuable experiences in my Christian life.

If finding a mentor is something you long for in your own life, remember that the Bible teaches us to be persistent and specific in prayer. While you're waiting and hoping, do not lose heart or feel you can't go on without a mentor; we all have the most incredible mentor of all to lean on—the precious Holy Spirit, the Counselor, who breathes hope, joy and wisdom into us.

The Woman in Proverbs 31

There are many different types of women in the Bible. We meet the manipulative, the scheming, the bitter, the deceitful ones—

all those are women we don't want to be like. But then there are the bold, godly, wise and pure ones who we're keen to imitate—characters like Esther, Ruth, Anna and Mary. These women overcame, persevered and glorified God. Because of that, their reputations still shine and glorify Him today.

One woman whose life shines and inspires is the woman from Proverbs 31. Here King Lemuel recounts the message his mother taught him: how he was wanted and loved and how she desires for him not to waste his life on futile things but to aspire to kindness, justice and mercy. King Lemuel's mother finishes by painting a picture of the sort of woman he should look for: the one who surpasses all other women. In character and heart, dedication, and determination, this woman rises above the rest and gives all of us who are without role models a godly woman to emulate and to aspire to be:

A wife of noble character who can find?

She is worth far more than rubies.

Her husband has full confidence in her and lacks nothing of value.

She brings him good, not harm, all the days of her life.

She selects wool and flax and works with eager hands.

She is like the merchant ships, bringing her food from afar.

She gets up while it is still dark; she provides food for her family and portions for her servant girls.

She considers a field and buys it; out of her earnings she plants a vineyard.

She sets about her work vigorously; her arms are strong for her tasks.

She sees that her trading is profitable, and her lamp does not go out at night.

In her hand she holds the distaff and grasps the spindle with her fingers.

She opens her arms to the poor and extends her hands to the needy.

When it snows, she has no fear for her household; for all of them are clothed in scarlet.

She makes coverings for her bed; she is clothed in fine linen and purple.

Her husband is respected at the city gate, where he takes his seat among the elders of the land.

She makes linen garments and sells them, and supplies the merchants with sashes.

She is clothed with strength and dignity; she can laugh at the days to come.

She speaks with wisdom, and faithful instruction is on her tongue.

She watches over the affairs of her household and does not eat the bread of idleness.

Her children arise and call her blessed; her husband also, and he praises her:

"Many women do noble things, but you surpass them all."

Charm is deceptive, and beauty is fleeting; but a woman who fears the LORD is to be praised.

Give her the reward she has earned, and let her works bring her praise at the city gate (Prov. 31:10-31).

As we read this passage and follow its detailed description of this woman's nature and deeds, her reputation shines; this is a woman with a life, a heart, a family and a career—she's got the whole package. God is at the center of her life. The wisdom she has stored up, her enduring attitude and the kindness she has clothed herself in mean she's a joy to be around. In the next two chapters, we'll delve further into her God-given qualities for insight and inspiration.

I want to be like her! I think I've just found my new mentor!

Chapter 6

I Want to Be Like Her –
Part 2

Putting the Woman in Proverbs 31
Under the Microscope!

As we put this Proverbs 31 woman under the microscope, we find many inspiring qualities that make her such a beautiful role model and woman of God.

She Has No Fear
In terms of anxiety and worry, many of us would love to be like this woman!

> When it snows, she has no fear for her household; for all of them are clothed in scarlet. She makes coverings for her beds . . . she can laugh at the days to come (vv. 21-22,25).

The woman in Proverbs 31 fully understands that the harsh conditions of winter can cause devastation to her family and her livelihood; however, she is not worried or afraid. She is wise enough to have made preparations for her household, should the weather turn (bed coverings and warm clothes). She makes ready—and then chooses not to fear.

Even today in Britain and elsewhere where winter is severe, snow can be both chaotic and dangerous. It blocks roads, it freezes our central heating systems, and along with this can come a range of health risks. As the temperature drops and our bodies become subject to the stress of the cold, flu can spread and, in those who are vulnerable, ordinary viruses can lead to bronchitis and pneumonia. People are more likely to suffer heart attacks in very cold weather. The wise learn to take the necessary steps to get through a cold snap successfully—salt for the roads, spare electric heaters, warm clothes, and perhaps even a flu shot.

Fear and worry steal the peace and joy God has called us to live under.

Fear and worry steal the peace and joy God has called us to live under. But can we really have peace in a world of rape, theft, assault, death, sickness, terrorism, abduction, pedophilia and every other sin and uncertainty that hangs over us daily? How can we live in peace when any moment something terrible could happen to us or to the people we love?

Fear of tomorrow, though, can torment and destroy. Back in 2001, along with many others, I watched on television the terrible terrorist attacks on the Twin Towers in New York. Just three days later, I nervously boarded a plane to the United States. In those few hours on board, I realized just how much life can lead us to existing in a caged, terrified climate of "What if?" and "What's next?"

In Matthew 6, Jesus gives His Sermon on the Mount. He starts off with the Beatitudes, issuing guidelines and wisdom for right and godly living. Just after He finishes talking about the poor, He issues this powerful command:

> Therefore I tell you, do not worry about your life, what
> you will eat or drink; or about your body, what you will
> wear. Who of you by worrying can add a single hour to
> his life? But seek first his kingdom and his righteous-
> ness, and all these things will be given to you as well.
> Therefore do not worry about tomorrow, for tomorrow
> will worry about itself. Each day has enough trouble of
> its own (vv. 25,27,33-34).

Jesus' teaching is not a chilled out hippy message along the
lines of "no worries, man," but a call to trust and seek God. The
Bible tells us lovingly and with great authority that our times are
in His hands—and we must entrust to those very same hands the
things we hold dearest.

At a women's Bible study recently, the topic turned to the
subject of fear and how the irrational "what ifs?" can bind many
to living a very different, small life. Since that journey in
September 2001, my fear of flying became progressively worse—
to the stage, in fact, where it was stopping me from going to
places I felt God had called me to go. During this Bible study,
there was a powerful time of prayer. I really felt God freeing me
and giving me back peace and confidence. Just a few weeks later,
as I boarded a plane, I remembered that beautiful and encourag-
ing line from the courageous woman in Proverbs 31: "she can
laugh at the days to come" (v. 25).

She Is Busy, Diligent and Disciplined

> She selects wool and flax and works with eager hands.
> She is like the merchant ships, bringing her food from

afar. She gets up while it is still dark; she provides food for her family and portions for her servant girls. She considers a field and buys it; out of her earnings she plants a vineyard. She sets about her work vigorously; her arms are strong for her tasks. She sees that her trading is profitable, and her lamp does not go out at night. In her hand she holds the distaff and grasps the spindle with her fingers (Prov. 31:13-19).

This woman is multitalented; she makes clothes and bedding for her family, and she's also the budding entrepreneur because she sells the rest of the garments (see v. 24). She is the ultimate practical woman!

I used to find it hard to relate to women with such endless practical talents, because I am just not like that. It's not simply that I can't sew or knit, but neither am I motivated to learn to do these things. Nor am I the kind of woman who is flushed with excitement at the prospect of sharing her chocolate brownie recipe with the Bible study group. I'd rather buy ready-made cakes!

If you are practical-minded, you'll probably find this virtuous wife easier to relate to than I initially did. But it is not just a question of *what* this woman does but the *spirit* in which she does it. Whatever she does, she does it to a high standard. She seems to have a wonderful sense of balance—an eye for quality but also a sense of responsibility with her money. If she shopped today, she would probably buy the top-of-the line name brands *and* the generic brands at the grocery store! In clothing, she doesn't do *just* designer or *just* budget—but is apparently a good steward, knowing when to feast and when to fast!

It's easy to envy a woman with a full life. She makes it look so effortless—she juggles commitments without looking frazzled and she seems to work hard but without excessive striving. Many statistics and surveys show that working mothers and high-flying career women are the most stressed of all categories of people. I've met a few women who are trying desperately "to have it all" yet are finding there are not enough hours in the day. But this passage in Proverbs gives us some hope—this woman manages to be a wife, a mother, a homemaker and a businesswoman! She seems to be successful in juggling a very busy life. So what is her secret?

I believe her secret lies in the beauty of her hard-working spirit. She may be gifted as a mother and a homemaker, but my guess is her days are *not* as smooth-running and effortless as the passage seems to imply. My feeling is that her secret is that she works with great effort. She is not a complainer or a slacker. She has realized that to get through everything and run her life well, she must work hard and be disciplined.

I have worked with many wonderful Christian leaders and have come to learn that in many cases the reason they lead so well and have been trusted with so much is that they have learned the art of personal discipline. It is not just what you see up front—it is also what they have cultivated behind the scenes. Their "quiet place" has prepared them for the impressive work that makes many feel in awe of them. How can they do that job with children? How can they run that office so smoothly? Where did that knowledge of the Bible come from? Usually, it is the *unseen* hours that are the key; they use their time and lives wisely.

If my children are late for school, if my Bible study is rushed or unfinished, or if I haven't returned people's phone calls, it is sometimes because I like to rest a little too much! I know it is my weakness, and I know it will be one of the main things that might stop me from fulfilling my purpose. If, like me, you want the big beautiful life that this woman in Proverbs 31 had in such fullness, then we both need to recognize that it was not achieved effortlessly. She probably sacrificed sleep, rest and relaxation, but she gained peace, harmony, identity, godliness and a happy home.

A wise woman once told me, "Mark your life by having a disciplined routine." Her personal rule was "in at eleven, up at seven." In other words, be wise, sleep well, and set your alarm! Like the woman in Proverbs 31, we need to make disciplined choices: "She . . . does not eat the bread of idleness" (v. 27). Laziness results in bitter consequences and a chaotic home. If we want to be trusted with much, we must adopt a hard-working attitude. God can change our hearts and our laziest habits. Just look at all that this woman achieves simply by mastering a disciplined routine. I may feel I cannot cope, but the more I order my life, the more room there is for God.

Be busy and organized, but don't strive to give the impression of a perfectly run life.

As in most things, though, balance, of course, is the key. Just as some of us have a tendency to be lazy, others will try to drive themselves into the ground with their unrealistic expectations of themselves. Be busy and organized, but don't strive to give the impression of a perfectly run life if, in fact, you are feeling totally burnt-out and miserable. We need to work hard, but adequate rest is just as important.

I Want to Be Like Her – Part 3

The Beautiful Nature of the Woman in Proverbs 31

This woman not only masters physical hard work, but she also disciplines her tongue in the same way. As we know from the passage, she is both an employer with servants and a woman with children. But how does she lead those in her care? Does she rule in a fierce, dominant way? Does she have to lose her temper or deliver punishments in order to be obeyed? What is her style?

Her beautiful nature allows her to lead firmly but in a way that is a blessing both to her family and to her servants. She is very much in control, yet she leads with kindness and gentleness. She does not need to resort to anger or screaming to bring her house and her affairs under her control:

She speaks with wisdom, and faithful instruction is on her tongue . . . her children arise and call her blessed; her husband also, and he praises her: "Many women do noble things, but you surpass them all" (Prov. 31:26,28-29).

How difficult it is to follow someone, or to be parented by someone, whose standards are too high and harsh—the person who demands much but issues instructions unkindly. But this woman is both easy to follow and easy to respect. She does not bark or yell commands, nor does she demand authority. She leads in a way that is a blessing to follow—in kindness and wisdom.

Colossians 3:20 says, "Children, obey your parents in everything, for this pleases the Lord," and verse 21 says, "Fathers, do not embitter your children, or they will become discouraged." Similarly, we read in Colossians 4:1: "Masters, provide your slaves with what is right and fair, because you know that you also have a Master in heaven."

How difficult it is to follow someone, or to be parented by someone, whose standards are too high and harsh.

The woman in Proverbs 31 seems to apply both these biblical principles: She is in authority, yet easy to obey. Not only that, but her household does not need to rebel. They are blessed by her godly approach, and as a result they esteem, love and bless her publicly. Her stunning parenting methods have brought her a great reward.

Anyone who is a daughter, parent, leader or boss knows that at times it is impossible to be listened to. I know in my house that sometimes I have to ask over and over again before the simplest task will be completed. Each time I'm ignored, my demand becomes more fierce—and before long I'm sure I can be heard "repeating my demand" in the next street!

We may have witnessed for ourselves parenting that has been mostly made up of nagging, screeching and angry demands, but as I read this passage I realize that although shouting may get a response, it doesn't result in my household feeling loved or well-led. This woman is a great example of a strong leader and a wonderful mother. The authority she has is marked by gentleness, and that is what makes her effective in her role. She disciplines and gives instruction without scarring those under her or making them feel that they have been sinned against.

In our lives, we may sometimes have to parent willful off-spring or lead difficult people. Rather than letting this ruin us (or damage them), we can learn from this wonderful woman's life how to take control and lead in a calm and consistent way. Our present methods may get a certain kind of result, but I believe this woman's style of doing things is God's preferred way for us and for those under our care.

Another reason that this woman has managed to achieve such a perfect style of leadership may be due to another of her beautiful attributes: wisdom. Leadership, marriage and parenting all require huge amounts of wisdom—almost supernatural wisdom! Wisdom is needed when we suddenly find ourselves out of our depth, and our brand-new "gentle" approach quickly turns to anger and frustration. God is kind enough to offer this gift of wisdom freely—all we need to do is ask: "If any of you lacks wisdom, he should ask God, who gives generously to all without finding fault, and it will be given to him" (Jas. 1:5).

Many of the women whom others model themselves after, and who have become icons in the world of fame and fashion, earn their living and their reputation simply with what we see on the outside: their veneer. In reality, we know nothing about their true nature or personality. We see them in magazines and films, but we do not know them. The only beauty that the media want us to see is their outward appearance, but that image will one day fade. What will those with little other than physical beauty leave behind?

Our friend in Proverbs 31 leaves her legacy by allowing us to know her through the Bible. She has no veneer, only depth of character and a stunning inner beauty. She is a kind and caring woman whose words are not her own, but are learned from God. She is feminine and dresses herself in the finest linen, yet there is nothing to indicate she is materialistic or concerned with outward appearances. She takes pride in her womanhood without losing sight of what is truly important: inner beauty. She captures the essence of woman and captivates others. She is worth "far more than rubies" (v. 10) and "she brings . . . good, not harm, all the days of her life" (v. 12). She is in spirit and nature everything that I long to be as a woman.

What will those with little other than physical beauty leave behind?

So how has she become so beautiful within and spiritually rich? Proverbs 31 ends by saying, "Charm is deceptive, and beauty is fleeting; but a woman who fears the LORD is to be praised. Give her the reward she has earned, and let her works bring her praise at the city gate" (vv. 30-31). Her God has been her resource, her inspiration, her wisdom. She has put Him first and so has become more like Him. He is the One who brings about her good name and causes her to do good deeds. Just as "the fear of the LORD is the beginning of wisdom" (Prov. 9:10), her fear of the Lord is why she has become so greatly admired. It is her worship of God that has cultivated such a praiseworthy life.

Perhaps the standards of the woman in Proverbs 31 make you feel defensive. Perhaps you think this is just a little too sweet and perfect. The good news is that as we bring our inadequate lives before God, He *increases* and we *decrease*. We hope we will become more like her along the way, but all the time we are ultimately becoming like Him if we keep His commands. So as we look at the life of the woman in Proverbs 31, let's not worship what appears to be unobtainable perfection—but instead vow to continue worshiping God, who, through His gift to us of the sacrifice at the cross, enables us to die to the old and become new creations. We are women made to bring Him praise!

Chapter 8

I Want to Break the Cycle

Many of us have a deep longing to be women of God, but before we can fully take hold of this calling, we need to break free of some of the destructive addictions and life patterns that dominate our lives. In other words, we have to break the cycle. Some of us might even be living in a cycle that has been repeated throughout several generations of our family. Others of us have a certain life habit that we constantly struggle with and cannot seem to break free of on our own. The good news is that in Christ we can be free. Colossians 3:1-3 is an amazing piece of truth for those of us who desire to break the cycle of destructive ways:

> Since, then, you have been raised with Christ, set your hearts on things above, where Christ is seated at the right hand of God. Set your minds on things above, not on earthly things. For you died, and your life is now hidden with Christ in God.

In other words, the good news has happened—newness and freedom in Christ. We've been raised up with Jesus. But now we must make some good choices in order to live and walk in the reality of this truth—we must set our minds on the things above.

As Paul reminds us a few verses later, we take off the old self and put on the new self (see vv. 9-10).

For the rest of this chapter, I'm going to leave you in the very capable hands of my good friend Irene Brooks. Irene is a trained counselor, has a great gift for teaching in this area, and has an excellent track record in helping many people (including me!) talk about these issues and pray through them. Her teaching outlined below is a gold mine of biblical and practical wisdom; it contains, quite honestly, some of the most powerful insights in this area that I've ever come across. I also feel really indebted to Irene for sharing so much with us here about the problems she had prior to becoming a Christian.

So, over to you, Irene!

• •

This chapter is about overcoming bad habits and addictions, but before we race ahead, let's remind ourselves of something very important: God loves us anyway! No matter how bound up we are in bad habits, Jesus loves us as passionately now as He did when He died for us (see Rom. 5:8). He is not waiting for us to "get better" so that He can love us more. We may not be enjoying all the good things He has for us yet, but His love for us is as strong and sure as it ever was (see Rom. 8:37–39) and He's rooting for us all the time (see Heb. 7:25). His love will help us find our way through the most stubborn problems as long as we hang in there and keep trusting Him for His help.

Bad Habits

Any negative behavior we can't break is a bad habit, and bad habits, if not curbed, can easily become addictions. Addictions may relieve our pain temporarily, but they always make us feel worse in the end. Jesus wants us to be free of life-controlling habits. "But how?" we cry, as we reach for the next blueberry muffin!

When I became a Christian, I was addicted to alcohol, cigarettes and a number of other very bad behaviors. Some of my problems fell away immediately after I handed my life over to Jesus, but others have taken time and hard work to overcome. Even now, I know there are things in my life that God wants me to overcome.

If you are struggling with patterns of behavior that keep defeating you, it will help first of all to understand how these patterns develop. Later, we will look at the addiction cycle and how to break out of it.

Good Habits

Anyone who has learned to drive a car, play a musical instrument (or a sport), or even to brush his or her teeth regularly did so because God has built into us a wonderful capacity to form habits. A habit, roughly speaking, is any behavior we repeat automatically without thinking about it. Obviously, some habits are good for us, while others—like eating too much or shouting whenever we get angry—are bad. The good news is that because habits are learned, they can also be *un*learned—and that includes even very bad, long-term habits and addictions.

If a habit develops because we stop thinking about what we are doing, then part of breaking a habit means learning to think again about what we *are* doing. The other part involves *choosing* to do something different. That's the best way to break a bad habit: Do something that you value more instead.

"That's too easy," I can hear you say—and yes, in part, you're right. But that *is* the gist of it. As we go along, we will unpack each stage of the process so that we can better understand how to make this process actually happen. In the meantime, remember: *If you want to break a bad habit, do something you value more instead.*

When I first became a Christian, my relationship with my then-boyfriend abruptly died. He didn't want to believe in God and go to church—and I did. I developed a different lifestyle. Before long, there wasn't room in my life for him any more, and we split up. I didn't want to hang around drinking myself into oblivion and doing things I now knew were shameful. My heart had changed, and I wanted to please God with everything within me. The more time I spent with Jesus and His people, the more I wanted to know Him and please Him.

Of course, these feelings are not always so strong, and my motivation sinks low at times. But in the deepest places of my heart, I want God more than anything, because when I started my new life with Him, God took out my old stony heart and gave me a new one that knows Him, loves Him and wants to do His will (see Jer. 31:33). When we break bad habits, it's important that we do it because we love God, and not just to get out of the problems it causes us. If our hearts are not set first on pleasing God, our good intentions will not last and we will slide back into bad patterns of behavior.

The Power of the Holy Spirit

"But how?" you might ask. "I know I love God, but I still do the things I know I shouldn't." And this is the next key point. If we truly follow Jesus, our hearts are changed and we are filled with God's Holy Spirit. He is the Change Agent that God has given us. He is the One who will help us lead clean and holy lives. He is the One "who works in us to will and to act according to his good purpose" (Phil. 2:13).

Charles Wesley, the great hymn writer, put it like this: "By faith we receive the Holy Spirit, which is of God, to replace the spirit of the world which is in us . . . This Holy Spirit—Christ in us—is that great gift which, at various times and in various manners, God has promised." And Oswald Chambers, another great man of God, said: "Before we can love God we must have the Lover of God in us, namely, the Holy Spirit."

> *If our hearts are not set first on pleasing God, our good intentions will not last and we will slide back into bad patterns of behavior.*

God knows our weaknesses, and it is for this very reason that He has given us the Holy Spirit to help us. Jesus told us that without Him we can do nothing (see John 15:5)—we cannot change ourselves, we cannot make ourselves better, we cannot overcome our weaknesses.

The Cycle of Addiction

When a habit becomes an addiction, it means that this habit has become life-controlling to the point where it may actually threaten our lives. We often see this graphically in the misuse of drugs or alcohol. Addictions cause ever-increasing degrees of chaos, pain and loss in every area of our lives: relationships, work, family, finances, appearance, leisure, and health of body and mind. Therefore, when a bad habit becomes a life-controlling addiction, we have to develop an entirely new lifestyle to break free from it. The following diagram shows how the addiction cycle develops.

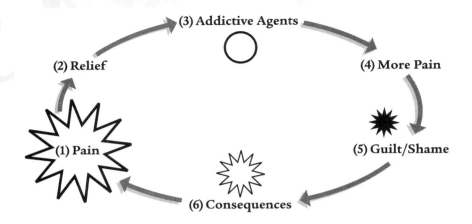

The addiction cycle starts with pain, which could be physical or emotional, or both (1). Pain makes us search for relief (2) through our favorite addiction (3). This is usually some substance or some activity that will either dull the pain or distract us long enough to forget about it temporarily.

But the anesthetic or distracting effect of our addiction only lasts for a short time before more pain (4) comes flooding back. It is now compounded with feelings of guilt and shame (5) as we are faced with the consequences of our behavior (6). This usually involves losses of finances, friendship and our future, as well as loss of face. This leads us right back to the beginning of the cycle—and yet more pain (1). This cyclical repetition of addictive behavior will continue unless we take drastic steps to break out of it and cultivate new, healthy behaviors instead.

Before going any further, let's have a look in turn at each of these stages of addiction.

Stage 1: Pain

Events in the present can remind us of painful incidents from the past—which is what usually kicks off the cycle in the first place.

This present-day event is often called "triggering" a past memory.

For instance, many of my own problems with depression and suicidal urges began with my angry, resentful reactions to my mother's rejection. She had a demeaning nickname for me, *Meitjie*, which is the Afrikaans word for a little servant girl. It could have been that she meant it affectionately, but her harsh demands for me to do very difficult household chores, when I was just a small child, made me resent her deeply. A meitjie was the lowest of the pile, the most despised and least desirable of the lowest of the classes in South Africa at the time. That is why I have always loathed all forms of racism, especially racist jokes.

And, yes, you guessed it—I developed a great big Cinderella complex! Oh, yes, I was extremely willing to take the servant role, not expecting anything for myself, but underneath I was seething with rage and rejection. It came to a head when my first husband decided he preferred men and left me on my own with two small children. I became so depressed that I very nearly managed to destroy my life.

Looking back, I now know that God saved me, even before I knew Him as my loving heavenly Father. I was into Buddhist meditation at this time, and one day, while I was meditating after a very serious suicide attempt, some words came into my mind, just as if someone was speaking to me: "Your life is not yours to throw away." From that moment on, I knew that I had no right to try to end my life, and somehow I managed to find other ways of dealing with the deep depression that swept over me from time to time.

Later on, we'll talk about the need to forgive the people who have hurt us, but in the meantime the first step in breaking the addiction cycle is for us to identify painful events in our past—and the anger that nearly always lurks underneath. Paul told the

Colossian Christians to rid themselves of "anger, rage, malice, slander and filthy language" (Col. 3:8), which he said was the problem behind their bad behavior, "sexual immorality, impurity, lust, evil desires and greed, which is idolatry" (v. 5).

Dealing with Anger

Christian women often deny their anger because they think it's wrong to be angry. But Paul told the Ephesian Christians, "Be angry and do not sin; do not let the sun go down on your anger" (Eph. 4:26, *ESV*). In other words, we must first admit we're angry and then we must put things right with the person we are angry with that very same day. When we don't sort things out as soon as possible, anger very quickly turns into resentment and becomes a root of bitterness (see Heb. 12:15). Jesus said anger stored up in our hearts is like murder (see Matt. 5:21-22).

Take time to think about everyone who has hurt you and made you angry. You can express your anger by using a journal. Set a time of 15 minutes and write down everything that comes into your mind concerning what has made you so angry. Don't stop writing until the timer rings. Don't censor what you write or check your spelling or grammar. Just write! God will not be offended by what you say—after all, He knows what's in your heart anyway. When you have finished (and it may take longer than 15 minutes!), ask God to forgive you and heal your heart. Forgive the person or people who have hurt you. Talk to your minister or a trusted friend if necessary and ask him or her to pray for you.

Stage 2: Relief

We all want instant relief from pain, and we often learn to deal with our pain by imitating the important people in our lives. My own mother had a problem with depression and anger, and she drank quite heavily. Consequently, that's how I too learned to deal with my bad feelings. My dad was a very mild-mannered man, always a safe refuge during the frequent storms in our family. Unfortunately, he never stood up for me against my mother—which I resented because she was physically abusive toward me. He would bury his bad feelings instead of tackling them directly. So I learned patterns of burying my feelings, ranting like my mother when I couldn't stuff them down any more, and anesthetizing the pain with alcohol, sexual sin and other forms of substance abuse.

Jesus has not promised us a pain-free life, but He has told us that He will never leave us nor forsake us (see Heb. 13:5). The writer to the Hebrews tells us that Jesus has compassion for us because He has been "touched with the feeling of our infirmities [weaknesses]" (4:15, *ASV*). Isaiah calls Jesus "a man of sorrows and familiar with suffering" (Isa. 53:3).

The following poem was written by a young woman when she realized that Jesus was with her, comforting her and sharing her pain while her mother abused her:

WERE YOU THERE? (ISAIAH 63:9)

Were you there at the first slap
When the plate crashed and the fist fell?
As I collapsed, was it your arms that I knew so well?
Were those all my tears or were they yours?
Sitting huddled in a puddle in the corner
Was it your lap I sat on?
Is that where you were?

Were you there, Abba?
When the needle pricked,

The lightning flicked,
As one hand held hair,
Did my other hand you grip?

Was your shadow present in the darkened room?
Did you see my foolishness, rejection, and sin?
Kneeling in agony, crying out in prayer,
Was your hand covering my disgrace?
Father, were you really there?

Were you there when it ended?
When hearts were split in two
Never again to be repaired
Unless they were to awaken and come to you.
Did you weep as vows were forgotten?
Jesus, was your heart breaking too?

You were there.
Soaring on your wings across the sea
I enter into a foreign, unknown land.
You release me into this place of rest
And in your grace and mercy I will forever stand.

Thank you for reminding me of your presence.
Your child.*

When we share our pain with Jesus and experience His comfort, we find it easier to forgive and let go of the hurt. We may still not understand why God has let us suffer, but we will know He cares. The cross teaches us that He is a God who has suffered the ultimate pain, not because He deserved to, but because it was the only way to pay the price for our sin and bring us back into His loving arms forever.

Stage 3: Addictive Agents

Addictions broadly involve two groups of behavior. First, there is *substance misuse*, which means ingesting substances that alter our mood, such as alcohol, drugs and food. Second, there is *performance addiction*. This also alters our mood, but it is achieved through activities such as overexercising, perfectionism, being a workaholic, or over-indulging in hobbies, sports or pastimes— such as watching TV, collecting, leisure pursuits, day-dreaming, religious rituals, shopping, and even swearing and shouting.

When we share our pain with Jesus and experience His comfort, we find it easier to forgive and let go of the hurt.

Jesus told a story about a lost son (the prodigal son) that vividly contrasts these two different kinds of addictive behaviors (see Luke 15:11-32). The younger brother was given his inheritance from his father and squandered it on wild living. In terms of putting this story into today's context, we might imagine that this involved drugs, sex and rock 'n' roll. In the original story in the Bible, the younger son ended up in a distant land, alone, penniless and feeding pigs in a foreigner's pigsty—not a nice ending for a respectable Jewish boy and the son of a wealthy father! Today, he might have been a freewheeling lawbreaker who hates rules, regulations and authority; someone who would do anything to feed his addiction.

But really there are *two* lost sons in the story, although the older brother didn't leave home to get caught up in sin. We first encounter him slaving away in his father's fields, angry and alone. He has deliberately shut himself out of his father's house to avoid his younger brother's noisy homecoming. This older son is so full of rage that his father can't believe it.

"My son," he pleads, "we *had* to celebrate and be glad, because this brother of yours was [as good as] dead and is alive again; he was lost and is found" (Luke 15:31-32, emphasis added).

The older brother is actually in a far worse state than the younger one—who at least had the grace to recognize his sin and come home repentant. The older brother, on the other hand, is so deceived by his outwardly good behavior that he can't see his need to repent. He thinks he is better than his younger sibling. But God doesn't look at the outward appearance of things—He looks at the heart underneath (see 1 Sam. 16:7). We see the older brother's heart in his bitter response to his father's kind invitation to join the party: He is full of jealousy, pride, rage and malice.

In some ways we could argue that the older son is typical of some performance addicts: They are dedicated to looking good on the outside, with behavior that is dutiful and self-sacrificing, but on the inside, they may be full of rage and hurt. Sadly, the older brother in the Bible story can't see his need to repent, and the passage ends with him just standing there, still mouthing off at his father outside the house.

Even though the younger son in this parable came home contrite and repentant, the father wouldn't hear a word of his contrition and didn't want him to grovel (see Luke 15:22-24). Today, the passage might have gone something like this:

> "Quick!" he shouted to the servants. "My boy's back! Send for the best take-out in town! We need champagne and party poppers. And get my best suit from the wardrobe and those new shoes I bought last week. I can't

have my son walking around like a barefoot slave!"

And to his son he might have said:

"And here, boy, take the family ring from my finger. No,
I insist! No son of mine belongs in the servants' quarters.
It doesn't matter what you've done—you're still my son!"

Can you imagine the father's hug? Can you see the son's
astonished face as the realization dawns on him that his father is
not furious with him? He might have said, "I deserve the worst,
but he's giving me the best! He's not shaming me, nor punishing
me for being so wicked, so foolish. He loves me! He really loves
me. I can't believe it—I'm still his son!"

I imagine there were many tears as father and son embraced
and made their peace. And the son saw a new side to his father—
one he had never seen before. Indelibly printed on his mind forever would be that look of delighted joy on his father's face in
that moment that they were reunited. He would know forever in
the deepest places of his heart that he was loved with a love as
"strong as death," a love "many waters cannot quench . . . [nor]
rivers wash . . . away" (Song of Songs 8:6-7).

Sadly, we can't tell from the Bible story what happened to
the older son. We have to leave him there, frozen in time, seemingly lost forever outside of the father's warm home and heart.
To him, the father was the harsh slave driver, and he was the
relentlessly driven son. His pride was a merciless jailer that kept
him locked out of the father's forgiving embrace.

If you recognize yourself in this story, don't let pride keep
you locked out of the Father's forgiveness, restoration and love.
If we confess our sins, God is "faithful and just and will forgive

us our sins and purify us from all unrighteousness" (1 John 1:9). That's one of the most wonderful promises in the whole Bible.

Stage 4: More Pain

People often talk about the heart being layered like an onion. Sometimes, it seems as if more recent pain in our lives beds itself down on previous layers, gradually building up a wound that resonates down from the present into the deepest layers of the past.

In my own life, the rejection I felt from my mother began at birth. I was the second of twins that were definitely *not* expected! After my brother was born and my poor mum almost died in the process, she was given the glad tidings that there was another baby in her womb, needing to be pushed out the same way— whereupon she passed out. Twenty-four hours later, she and the midwife finally got me out.

It's a long story, but there were no medical facilities in the wilds of Sri Lanka, where we were born. "The doctor thought we were all going to die," my mother used to tell us. "But we didn't; we all lived! But nobody knew you were there!" This last remark was always addressed to me, as if somehow it had all been my fault. In my childish ignorance, I interpreted this to mean that my brother was the expected baby, while I was the nasty surprise who nearly killed my mother by being born. I felt that I really should *not* have been there in the womb (nor here in the world), and people who cause so much trouble should not be allowed to live—unless, of course, they make up for it by being very, very good and always doing everything they are told to do.

It is unlikely that my mother intended for me to feel like this, but the difficulties I experienced with her over the ensuing years confirmed these deeply held beliefs. Of course, I was not conscious of these thoughts during my growing-up years and into my adulthood. They were deeply buried in my subconscious mind and only began to emerge after I became a Christian—as God began to heal my heart and set me free from this sense of rejection.

Everyone experiences rejection. God created us to enjoy warm, loving relationships, but Adam and Eve's fall plunged us all into broken relationships—with God, with others and with ourselves. The Bible is peppered with examples of rejection: Cain (Adam and Eve's first child) killed his brother out of a sense of jealous rejection; Jacob stole his brother's rights as the firstborn and spent the next 20 years fleeing his brother's rage; Joseph was nearly killed by his brothers' jealousy and rejection; and Jesus Himself was rejected and then crucified.

If you know you are vulnerable to feeling rejected, bring it to God and ask for His healing.

Over the centuries, many of His followers have lost their lives because they too were rejected because of their belief in Christ.

The story of the woman at the well is a good example of the layered effect of rejection (see John 4:1-42). Rejected by five previous husbands and now living in sin, she went to draw water in the heat of the day when most other women would have been at home feeding their families. Her sense of racial and religious rejection keeps showing up in her conversation with Jesus.

Rejection makes people sensitive and defensive. Sometimes they become shy and withdrawn or sharp and hostile—or even both. If you know you are vulnerable to feeling rejected, bring it to God and ask for His healing. When we look at self-image a little later, you will understand how His love heals us of this feeling of rejection.

Stage 5: Guilt/Shame

Adam's first reaction to his own sin was to hide (see Gen. 3:7-10). Guilt is that awful, gut-sinking feeling that we have done wrong, and it makes us want to hide. Shame goes one step further: It is that dreadful feeling that we have failed because there is something horribly wrong with us. With shame, we don't just want to hide; we also want to get away from the eyes that see us in our shamefulness and silence the voices that accuse us of wrongdoing. Shame often makes us blame others—this was Adam's second reaction. Beneath his guilt and shame, Adam felt like the victim of his circumstances. So did Cain. Rejected people feel like victims.

Adam did not take responsibility for his sin. When we hide and blame others out of guilt and shame, we too are not taking responsibility for our sin. We too are acting like victims. That doesn't mean that we are responsible for the way that others have sinned against us. God is not asking us to pretend that the wrong that others have done to us is unimportant.

My mother's rejection of me was wrong. I was a little girl who needed her mother's love and protection. Her cruel treatment and harsh words wounded me deeply. But before I could forgive her, I had to take responsibility for my own sinful reactions: my hatred and judgments against her. Before I could move on, I had to ask God to forgive me for the hatred stored up in my heart and my rejection of my mother. Feeling rejection can make us in turn reject others, and it breaks the cycle of love that God wants us to show to everyone—even the people who have hurt us.

Unfortunately, my mother died before I could make my peace with her. If she were alive today, I would try to talk to her about her rejection of me and how she hurt me. I would also ask her to forgive me for judging and hating her, for setting myself against her and never letting her into my heart. But although I can't speak to her any more, God has forgiven me for my sin toward her. He has also helped me grieve for my lost relationship with her. Now I can thank Him for her. I am grateful for the gift of life I received through her, for her strength of character, her determination, her strong sense of right and wrong, and the care she gave me as a child.

Many of us have problems of resentment toward our parents for things they have or have not done. Or our resentment may be toward an older brother, an uncle, a grandfather, a neighbor, a teacher or a gym coach. We may even have been victims of serious abuse. Before we can move on, we must get rid of the hatred in our hearts.

The fourth commandment tells us to honor our father and our mother; this commandment has a pivotal place between God's commandments about our relationship with Him and the rest of His commandments about our relationships with other people. Paul said that if we honor our parents, things will go well for us (see Eph. 6:2-3). On the other hand, the Old Testament talks of a curse on those who dishonor their fathers and mothers (see Deut. 27:16). Bad attitudes toward our parents, whatever our parents may have done to us, will spoil our relationship with God and others.

Forgiveness is a hard step to take, but it is worth it. You will feel the love and peace of God like never before! Start by being honest about your feelings. Face the fact that some people have wronged you and that you are angry, hurt, disappointed—whatever is true for you. At the same time, let go of your right to judge them. The Bible says: "Do not repay anyone evil for evil. Do not take revenge . . . but leave room for God's wrath . . . 'It is mine to avenge; I will repay,' says the Lord" (Rom. 12:17,19). God is asking us to be real about the sin, but to leave the sinner in His hands. He alone knows everything, and He alone is wise and loving enough to judge others. We are not. This is what forgiveness is all about: being real about what has happened but letting go of the right to judge.

We also need to be wise about whether it is right to seek reconciliation with the person who has wronged us. God does not want us to put ourselves at risk by trying to befriend an abuser who has not repented. Nor does forgiveness mean that the normal processes of law should not take place. If someone has broken the law, it may be necessary to report him or her to the proper authorities.

We have to realize that hiding and blaming don't work; they only make matters worse. Instead, we must go straight to God with our guilt and shame. If other people have shamed us, we must forgive them and allow God to heal our hearts.

Stage 6: Consequences

Bad habits and addictions lead to multiple losses in many areas of life. It may take time for this to show, but if we sow the wind, we *will* reap the whirlwind (see Hos. 8:7). Paul told the Galatians, "A man reaps what he sows. The one who sows to please his sinful nature, from that nature will reap destruction; the one who sows to please the Spirit, from the Spirit will reap eternal life" (Gal. 6:7-8).

Let's follow the steps above and make up our minds to break out of the addiction cycle. If you need extra help, make sure you get it from someone who knows what he or she is doing and who will work with you for as long as it takes.

Breaking the Addiction Cycle

Put Off . . . Put On

As mentioned earlier, to successfully break a bad habit or an addiction, we must not just concentrate on stopping certain behaviors.

In fact, that kind of strategy can sometimes work against us. That is why dieting, for example, so often backfires. We get obsessed with eating and—guess what—the temptation gets even stronger. Instead of focusing our attention on what we should *not* be eating, we need to teach ourselves to enjoy the foods that are good for us. We can make choices to eat differently, more healthily. That, along with healthy exercise and the cultivation of other hobbies, pastimes and activities that hold our attention, will help us not to become obsessed with food fads and diets.

We need to think about the consequences of our negative behavior and then decide instead to do other things that will be more rewarding and satisfying.

The same is true of any bad habit we are trying to break. We need to think about the consequences of our negative behavior and then decide instead to do other things that will be more rewarding and satisfying. Paul told the Galatians to "put on Christ" (Gal. 3:27, *ASV*), and the Ephesians to "put off your old self . . . and . . . put on the new self, created to be like God in true righteousness and holiness" (Eph. 4:22,24). But Paul's most beautiful exhortation was to the Colossians when he wrote:

> Therefore, as God's chosen people, holy and dearly loved, clothe yourselves with compassion, kindness, humility, gentleness and patience. Bear with each other and forgive whatever grievances you may have against one another. Forgive as the Lord forgave you. And over all these virtues put on love, which binds them all together in perfect unity. Let the peace of Christ rule in

your hearts, since as members of one body you were called to peace. And be thankful. Let the word of Christ dwell in you (Col. 3:12-16).

Imagine being like that: compassionate, kind, humble, gentle, patient, forgiving, loving, peaceful and thankful! It strikes me that these qualities have a lot to do with our attitudes toward other people. Addictions, on the other hand, are all about *us*—meeting *our* needs, fulfilling *our* desires.

A Change of Lifestyle

To break very serious addictions like alcoholism, continuous sexual sin, serious substance misuse and so on, we will have to change our lifestyle completely. This starts by finding a place where we have no access to the addictive substance or activity at all—at least for a while. Detox and rehab programs can provide a safe place to make a complete break with a destructive lifestyle. We may have to find a new place to live, a new job perhaps, and develop new friendships that have nothing to do with our addictive lifestyle. There is no easy way out of this; radical changes are needed to break an addictive lifestyle.

If this is true for you, look for the special help you need to make a fresh start. If you belong to a Christian fellowship, I am sure they will help you all they can. But, in the end, no one can do the hard work for you. But walk in grace—and note that a *relapse* does not have to be a *collapse*. Instead, it can be an opportunity for you to pick yourself up, dust yourself off, and start all over again. Work out what went wrong and get right back in there, breaking out of the addiction cycle.

Rejected people are *self*-rejecting. They usually define themselves in terms of their hurts and live out of a negative self-image. They suffer great pain—unnecessary pain. All it does is keep them locked into the addiction cycle.

To go back to my own story briefly, the fact that I ended up in a suicidal depression after my first marriage failed was largely because I believed so many lies about myself. That old rejection wound surfaced with a vengeance and fed my thoughts: *I am such an awful woman; it is* all my fault *our marriage has broken down. Who would want to live with a woman like me, anyway? People who cause so much trouble should really not be allowed to live. The world would be a much better place without me.* Of course, I know now that none of this is true, but I didn't know it then. How tragic to think it nearly cost me my life.

It's so important that we take time to discover the negative messages that are driving us into destructive behavior. Take a little time to think about your deepest hurts. What conclusions did you come to about yourself, other people, life and God? You may want to use journal entries in the way suggested before, freely expressing whatever is in your heart. You may want to map out a time line of your life and draw pictures of what home felt like—or school, or that awful man next door, or the kids who bullied you in class, or the teacher who said such horrible things about you.

Then you must repent of hating, judging and rejecting yourself. We must not reject what God has accepted or curse what God has blessed.

Know the Truth

Our identity is no longer defined by our past hurts, our circumstances, our race or color, what others have said about us, or even what we believe about ourselves. We are God's children now. He defines our identity, and He has some wonderful things to say about us. We are His treasured possessions, the apple of

His eye. He will never stop doing us good, day and night.

It is important to realize that as God's children, we are secure forever in a love that gave the best when we deserved the worst. Our worth in God's eyes is not measured by how clever, pretty or popular we are. Jesus gave His life for us—you and me. Our significance, destiny, importance and purpose are 100 percent bound up in God's plans for us: plans to prosper us and not to harm us, plans to give us a hope and a future (see Jer. 29:11).

These are the three roots of our identity: our need for security, self-worth and a sense of significance. Rooted and grounded in the love of Christ, we can stand firm in the most difficult times and grow strong throughout the passing season of life.

Take time to think about your security in the love of God, your self-worth in the blood of Christ, and the significance of your life in the purposes that God has *for you*. Find verses that confirm these three roots of your identity. There are many. Learn them by heart. Write songs about them. Thank your heavenly Father daily for His everlasting love, value and purposes for you. No matter what's happening in your life, your identity in God will never change. This is what the younger brother discovered in the story of the prodigal son. It didn't matter what he'd done—he was still his father's son.

Deal with Compulsive Thoughts

Our thoughts have powerful control over our feelings and behavior. Paul told the Corinthians to "take captive every thought to make it obedient to Christ" (2 Cor. 10:5). On another occasion he told the Christians in Rome to be changed by renewing their minds (see Rom. 12:2). What Paul meant is that we must take control over our thoughts and not allow them to run away with us. In some respects, our minds are like little children that have to be taught to be obedient, to behave in an orderly manner and not to run wild all over the place. He is telling the people that they must take control of their thinking so that they can live confident, productive lives in God.

This is very good news for us because it means that we too can make sure our thinking is positive, faith-filled and honoring to God. Proverbs 23:7 says, "As [a man] thinks within himself, so he is" (*NASB*). If we want to live good lives, we must train our minds to agree with God's Word.

Philippians 4:8 says, "Finally, brothers [and sisters!], whatever is true, whatever is noble, whatever is right, whatever is pure, whatever is lovely, whatever is admirable—if anything is excellent or praiseworthy—think about such things." It takes many years to train a child in the way he or she should go. The same is true of our minds. Learning God's Word by heart, thinking about it during the day and at night, singing songs full of truth, reading the Bible regularly and praying the words of Scripture back to God are some of the ways we can get to know the Word of God. If we are lazy and slack about God's Word, we are like the man in Proverbs who was too lazy to mend his garden walls. Robbers laid waste to his vegetable patch and spoiled his flowers (see Prov. 24:30-34).

"Catch . . . the Little Foxes"

Sometimes we stay stuck in destructive behavior because there are spiritual powers at work behind the scenes. This may be due to our own sin, traumas from the past, or spiritual holds that have come down to us through our family line.

I needed special prayer and help to break the power of the name "Meitjie" over me. It had become like a curse that kept me locked into a negative self-image. If this is the case in your life, you also will probably need special help, so make sure you talk to your pastor so that he or she can direct you to someone who knows what he or she is doing and can help you to get free. Always remember, God wants His children to be free.

In Closing

In this chapter, we focused on the dynamics behind bad habits and addictions, how to deal with background issues, and how to break the addiction cycle. There are many books and ministries that offer help in specific areas such as eating disorders, alcohol and substance misuse, perfectionism, burnout, stress disorders, depressive states and compulsive disorders. It has not been my intention to try to duplicate that kind of detailed ministry, but simply to give some pointers on how we can free ourselves from things that might be holding us back.

It is possible to put off old destructive ways and put on new, Christlike behavior. We have the Spirit of God within us to make us clean, renew us and lead us into all truth. He knows us better than we know ourselves. And yet He loves us with a commitment and a passion that would stagger us if we could but grasp even a tiny measure of it. He is the One who breathed these beautiful words through Paul, the great apostle:

Now *to him who is able to do immeasurably more than all we ask* or imagine, according to his power that is at work within us, to him be glory in the church and in Christ Jesus throughout all generations, for ever and ever! Amen (Eph. 3:20-21, emphasis added).

Thank God that we are all caught up together in His immense care and love!

Chapter 9

I Want to Have a "Big Life"!

Therefore I have set my face like flint, and
I know I will not be put to shame.

ISAIAH 50:7

I really, really want God to use my life.

A little while ago, I stood in my kitchen and unloaded the dishwasher with frustration. I looked out of the window and thought of all my friends who were "out there," changing the world, while I was "in here" cleaning up my kids' breakfast. I prayed over and over again: *I want a big life! I want a big life! I want a big life!* I had what you might call a little "moment."

In the run-up to praying that prayer, I had gotten into a pattern of just waking up, getting through the day, and going to bed. I felt as if I were awake, but asleep. I was going through the motions without actually having a sense of purpose, destiny or vision. I had come to a crisis point. My life felt small and I was without a vision.

I know God has a purpose for all of us—people for us to love, affect and reach out to. Life can be bland yet busy, or full and fulfilling. It's all about choice. I had definitely gone to sleep—awake in body but dozing off in spirit. In that moment standing by the dishwasher, I realized that I was ready to dream again, to wake up and take hold of the big life that God has waiting for all who are willing to surrender themselves, grasp their dreams, and make use of every waking moment to fulfill His purposes.

My prayer for a big life wasn't coming from a sense of boredom. I wasn't despising my life or wanting to be someone else. It was just that I realized that God had a race marked out for me and I wasn't running it. I could see my Christian friends taking hold of God in their own races and making a difference. I felt as if I'd gotten lost in the busyness of being a mum and the limitations that this kind of routine can bring. I'd just stopped dreaming and gone into autopilot. Every day felt like Groundhog Day, and I'd gotten it into my head that I was entering into my ineffective phase of life.

As new mums, busy students and full-time workers—and those of us who feel we only just have time to rush to church, let alone anything else—we have to be aware that the more we take on, the more danger there is that we will forget to see God in all these tasks. I was missing out on the God-purpose that awaits even the busiest person—what the Bible calls making the most of every opportunity (see Col. 4:5). I'd lost my sense of identity, and that moment at the dishwasher was when I finally woke up. I quickly finished loading the dishes in the dishwasher and headed for the school gates with an entirely different attitude.

A healthy desire for a big life doesn't grow from a sense of boredom and a lack of contentment. It begins with a vision. Just because we're busy with children or work doesn't mean we have to die to the vision. Outside of work, children or whatever it is that takes all our time, we have to ask, "Am I fulfilled? Or are my passions and dreams lying dormant?" As we begin to open our eyes, see the need, notice people and pray, we begin once again to devote ourselves to running the race marked out for us—drawing on the power and strength of God to achieve immeasurably more than we ever could on our own. A life and a dream rooted in Christ, and seen in faith, can be lived out beyond anything we'd ever thought of or concocted for ourselves. A little person in a small town or tiny village can end up making a mark on history and affecting people's lives forever.

Nancy Alcorn

Last year, I met a remarkable woman, Nancy Alcorn, who recently celebrated her fiftieth birthday. Nancy has chosen to follow a dream and allow God to use her life to affect thousands of girls and young women. In 1983, Nancy opened a home for broken and hurting girls through an organization she pioneered called Mercy Ministries.

A native of Tennessee and a huge sports fan, Nancy had been reaching out to troubled young women since she was at college. A serious knee injury kept her from playing sports at the college level, but for five years she coached young women in her role as athletic director for Tennessee's correctional facility for juvenile delinquent girls. But as time passed, Nancy became frustrated with the system. She wasn't seeing enough changes and thought she might see more results if she worked with younger children. So she asked for, and received, a transfer to the State Department of Human Services, where she supervised foster-care placements in the Nashville, Tennessee, area. Nancy then went on to work with the Emergency Child Protection Services Unit, investigating charges of abuse and neglect.

While working there, Nancy heard about a Christian organization called Teen Challenge and began to do volunteer work for them. In this capacity, she saw how God's Word transformed people, and the positive results gave her a sense of hope that she hadn't felt for a long time. Nancy then took on the job of Director of Women for Teen Challenge, and two years later she visited some friends in Louisiana. She soon discovered that the Louisiana area had a huge need for people to work with troubled young women, and on her return to Nashville she couldn't stop thinking about this.

She started to dream of setting up a home for women aged 13 to 28—a home where these young women could receive help with their various problems from trained professionals, completely free of charge, for a period of about 6 months. Nancy realized that many of these young women had deep-rooted emotional problems that resulted in a range of social problems, and her vision was to deal with these root problems, not just the symptoms.

So many women have been deeply wounded by incest, rape, physical and sexual child abuse, and other tragic experiences, and Nancy dreamed of creating an environment in which some of these women could deal with past hurts, be relieved of guilt, and address the root causes of their problems—all the while surrounded by the love of Christ. So began the vision of Mercy Ministries.

Nancy took her vision to the board of Teen Challenge. They liked the idea of establishing a home in Louisiana—which would include an outreach to pregnant teenagers—but it wasn't part of their plans. So, with Teen Challenge's blessing and a $1,000 contribution, Nancy left Tennessee in January 1983 to launch a home on her own.

Initially, the impact of her decision overwhelmed her. "I was inundated with fear—I cried all the way through church on my first Sunday there," she says. But her fear was quickly replaced with an indescribable peace. "I believe God dropped into my heart a gift of faith, because from that point on it never occurred to me it wasn't going to work. It was just a matter of not quitting—of finding a way to do what everybody said could not be done."

Money began to trickle in, and Mercy Ministries was finally able to open its first home. Young women came into the program from all over Louisiana and other parts of the United States. The biblical philosophy that Nancy had learned at Teen Challenge was unfolding before her eyes: The power of Christ can change a life.

Eventually, Nancy wanted to expand the home, but she felt it wasn't right to take any of the government funding that had been offered to her. Instead, she believed God was asking her to rely on Him to meet the need. This happened in an incredible way when Nancy found herself seated next to a businessman on a flight. She told him about the ministry, and when they landed, he asked her for a brochure. A month later, the man called and said he hadn't been able to forget about Mercy Ministries. He explained that his mother had been raped and, as a result, he had been conceived. If there hadn't been a place for her to go, he would have been aborted. He went on to ask her how much she needed for the new home. When she told him that she needed $150,000, he said instantly, "You've got it." He gave the money anonymously, with no strings attached.

In 1990, Nancy felt God was calling her back to Nashville to establish a home there. So she moved, and for five years she traveled extensively to help raise funds for a new home for 40 women.

Her dream became a reality in 1995 when a $2 million facility was completed—entirely debt-free.

Since then, Mercy Ministries has opened two homes in Sydney, Australia, and is planning a third. In addition, Mercy Ministries is looking for property in New Zealand and is also currently renovating a home in St. Louis, Missouri, that was donated by Joyce Meyer Ministries. Other homes are in the United Kingdom, Los Angeles and Houston.

Nancy Alcorn saw a need and dedicated her life to living the big life that God had in mind for her, fulfilling the vision. Her faithfulness and obedience has made a lasting difference to thousands of girls' lives and their futures.

Mother Teresa

Another woman who said yes to a big life and demonstrated faithfulness and obedience in a powerful, extravagant way was Mother Teresa. As I read her life story, it struck me that she did not have to be obedient to the call God placed on her life. But she made herself available, boarded a train alone for Calcutta, and took up her cross and followed Jesus. From that moment on, her love for Jesus propelled her into an ever-growing vision for the poor of that city. It must have been frightening at times, isolating and infuriating—but this was what she had been called to do.

On one occasion, a cynical press reporter asked her, "Mother Teresa, isn't all you are doing just a drop in the ocean?" "Yes," she replied, "but the ocean is made up of many drops." A fantastic response, which drives home the point that the smallness we feel about our lives comes from within. Here was the big life, one that made a difference to thousands of people's existences. Mother Teresa comforted countless people and nursed many into the arms of Jesus for all eternity.

How are we going to use our lives? What are our dreams? The lives of these two women, Nancy Alcorn and Mother Teresa, show us that God takes the faithful dreamer and pours out the extraordinary blessing of a full life—a life that gives glory to Jesus and extravagant encouragement to others.

> For we are God's workmanship, created in Christ Jesus to do good works, *which God prepared in advance for us to do* (Eph. 2:10, emphasis added).

> Now to him who is able to do immeasurably more than all we ask or imagine, according to his power that is at work within us, to him be glory in the church and in Christ Jesus throughout all generations, for ever and ever! Amen (Eph. 3:20-21).

Jesus created and designed each of us with a destiny, a purpose and a plan. We have a simple choice to make: to live *the full life* He's prepared for us, or to take a smaller, less risky life. A big life is available to all believers, but it is usually marked by some costly characteristics: an unyielding devotion to Christ, a passion to make a difference, and the ability to sow and persevere in the most trying of situations. Ironically,

We have a simple choice to make: to live the full life that Christ has prepared for us, or to take a smaller, less risky life.

some of the fruit of having a big life can actually make our day-to-day existence feel small and uninteresting, as the big life may involve a lot of work and lots of waiting.

I recently read a story in a national newspaper about a woman in her 30s who dreamed of having a baby, yet she suddenly felt hemmed in and dissatisfied when her little bundle arrived. "Babies are boring," she declared in the article. This was not the experience she had expected it to be. The nappies, crying and endless feedings quickly became tedious and distasteful. She was not able to have the vision or the perseverance to stick it out until the next stage—to work for the dream, to wait a bit longer for it to develop and mature. So she packed her baby off to a nursery in search of a bigger life.

The very next day, there was another article written by several mums in response. A few vehemently disagreed with her views, but many, many more women agreed. Words like "unstimulated," "depressed," "despondent" and "disillusioned" filled the page— these women had run out of vision and no longer had the energy to nurture and work for the dream.

But for Christians, in all areas of life (not just motherhood), perseverance and focusing on the Creator of our vision will be the key to our holding out when times are tough and to our pressing on to receive the promise.

Let us run with perseverance the race marked out for us. Let us fix our eyes on Jesus, the author and perfecter of our faith (Heb. 12:1-2).

God has a race marked out for each one of us. We're all running in the same direction, but no one else can have our lane or the opportunities God is giving us. We are all unique. In Christianity there are no clones!

Recently, I listened with passion and enthusiasm to Donna Crouch, who was speaking at a conference in London. The title of her talk was "Escaping a Small Life—Stir Up the Woman Born for a Great Cause." It reminded me of Paul's words in 2 Corinthians 6:11-13, which in *THE MESSAGE* reads as follows:

> Dear, dear Corinthians, I can't tell you how much I long for you to enter this wide-open, spacious life. We didn't fence you in. The smallness you feel comes from within you. Your lives aren't small, but you're living them in a small way. I'm speaking as plainly as I can and with great affection. Open up your lives. Live openly and expansively!

This is the path that leads to an extraordinary life. Sometimes the journey may be hard, boring or even lonely—and we may think we've missed out on having a full life. But when we get a glimpse of God's perspective, we soon begin to realize that even the small bits are a crucial part of embracing the big, marvelous life God has given us.

I have always had a massive heart for young women. Five years ago, I was privileged to be offered the job of running an organization called Soul Sista. I really wanted to see these girls know Jesus more deeply and be set free from the many burdens and lies that held them back from living a full life before God. We set up conferences and training days, but I realized early on that seeing these girls grow and be healed would be just 5 percent of my job. To make it happen would require 95 percent hard work, organization and administration (as well as maintaining my first priorities, which were running my home and looking after our small children full time). To realize the dream took a lot of sacrifice and hard work! But did I want the big life or not?

Sometimes I wanted to escape the seeming smallness of my

everyday routine—washing, ironing, cleaning, making phone calls, organizing paperwork, arranging merchandise—and escape to a more glamorous life for the day. But I also knew that changing my *attitude* was the key to finding and fulfilling my purpose. We can either be prepared to work for the dream by waking up tomorrow with a sense of anticipation and gratitude, walking into our world and embracing all that's ahead of us, or simply miss it by grumbling at the potentially unexciting events of the day and settling for life without a dream.

I learned so much from Nancy Alcorn's story—her vision to set up another home in Nashville. Did she receive the dream straight away? No, she traveled extensively for five years before the funds were raised and the house in Nashville was built. The more vision she had, the more she had to work and wait for the dream.

Whatever our particular challenge looks like, for most of us there will be times of excruciating perseverance. We have to strive not to get discouraged. As the writer of Hebrews reminds us, we need to look back at all the faithful runners who kept going to win the prize. Remember them, remember Nancy, and in times of endurance, hold on to Jesus!

An extraordinary life comes with a price, and if we really want to live life to the fullest in Christ, it will take discipline, vision and endurance.

An extraordinary life comes with a price, and if we really want to live life to the fullest in Christ, it will take discipline, vision and endurance. I quite like the phrase "make hard work your slave." Whether our particular race is run in the home, the office or at the college desk, there will be a cost involved. For me, I know there is no point in being dramatic and whiny when it gets to 10 P.M. and I've still got lunches to pack, laundry to do or a Bible study to prepare. It *is* hard work, but we are brave women and we can multitask! We can shove a load in the washing machine, butter a sandwich and take stuff out of the dishwasher—all at the same time! Let's not waste time and energy being dramatic and frustrated; let's just get on with it with a grateful attitude and realize this busyness is part of the big life we asked for.

Habakkuk 2:2 encourages us to write down the vision. Proverbs 29:18 tells us that "where there is no vision, the people perish" (*KJV*). If we don't have a vision or a dream, we are not living our God life to the full. If we think of ourselves as insignificant cogs, then we have no vision. We've got to know who we are and what we're for. How do we do that? Think, ponder, pray, petition, write it down . . . go back to it and then live it out.

My vision is to do a great job with my kids and encourage the women God has put around me in my community. That won't happen overnight. I long for various projects to take off, but in the meantime about 10 of us meet once a month in my front room to pray and read the Bible together. I know one of my biggest flaws is a lack of patience. But even though my timing is terrible, God's is perfect, and I know that I've got to continue to sow and serve while I wait.

I have often heard frustrated worship leaders complain that they are stuck in a coffee shop instead of on the stage. Or heard a passionate preacher frustrated by his lack of opportunity. What God tells us all is to be humble and patient and to embrace what it takes to get us there.

Remember David in the fields patiently watching the sheep? And Jesus Himself was a carpenter for most of His adult life, faithfully getting ready for what God had in mind for Him. He was 30 when His public ministry finally began. Sometimes the making of us is in the waiting. Growing and realizing a dream can feel a little like watching the tide come in. Every time the waves get a little further in to the shore, they are pulled back out into the sea. This can go on and on for hours. It is sometimes tedious to watch. But if you look at the sand, more and more grains are being touched, soaked and covered each time.

It's easy to believe that having a big life is effortless for some people, but really it is a process of being patient and learning to persevere each time the waves knock us back; never doubting the progress and impact that each little splash forward is making, just like Mother Teresa so faithfully believed.

There is a time for everything and everything is beautiful in its time.

So do you want a big life? Maybe you are frustrated by the way things are, and the dreams that once burned brightly now lie dormant. You want to make a difference, have an impact and be used by God. Just by praying that prayer, you are on the road. But it will be a long journey, full of many different stages and seasons. There is a time for everything and everything is beautiful in its time. Trust God and don't become disillusioned by seasons of the ordinary. Work hard. Keep going. Be faithful. Be patient. You have made a beautiful choice!

Christ in You, the Hope of Glory

You've probably noticed by now that there's a whole lot of "I want to" going on in the chapter titles of this book: "I want to be an uncomplicated woman," "I want to have a big life," "I want to break the cycle." But as I've tried to convey, these are not the vain cries of a comfort-loving, pampered life. These are the desperate and passionate prayers of a generation of women on a mission to become powerful tools in the hands of their God. There's not a hint here of the distorted "I want" declarations we hear swirling around us in today's self-obsessed and painfully broken society: "I want to feel better about myself" or "I want to be a powerful woman" or "I want plastic surgery." This is a purer and more purposeful cry: "I want to be a *beautiful woman of God*."

Wanting to be an uncomplicated, free, affirmed and empowered woman of God is a beautiful vision for life. But in order for it to become reality, we must move on from simply "I" and take the all-important, final step. In this last chapter, we will focus on that missing piece. The Christian life is not you on your own, striving to make things happen by mere willpower, discipline or determination. Instead, it is something far more glorious: "Christ in you, the hope of glory" (Col. 1:27).

As my Bible-teaching friend Louie Giglio often reminds people, it's not "Christ *and* you, the hope of glory"—like some wrestling partnership, whereby every time you grow tired of the assaults, Jesus comes into the ring to give you some recovery time and then hands everything back to you to try feebly again. It's not even just "Christ *with* you." He undoubtedly *is* with you, but too many of us have fallen for the "God is my co-pilot" sticker campaign, whereby ultimately we're still in charge of the controls and He's just giving us some incidental advice on navigating through this life. No, the beautiful news is this: It's "Christ *in* you, the hope of glory." The gloriously strong Maker and Sustainer of the universe is living in you—through the power of His Holy Spirit.

The Christian life is not you on your own, striving to make things happen by mere willpower, discipline or determination.

Think about that for a moment. The very same God who time after time led His people to win the day is living in and through *you;* who, through Moses, led the people of God out of slavery and into freedom; who spoke powerfully through Deborah the prophetess; who favored the lives of Esther, Daniel and Joseph in their high-profile positions; who gave strength to Samson and incredible victory to the shepherd boy David; who performed powerful acts and miracles through the apostles and those who followed in their example. This very same God lives in *you*—continuously breathing His power in and through you to give birth to a godly life. Amazingly, the very same Holy Spirit of God who empowered Jesus for His perfect earthly ministry is now dwelling inside of you.

We live in a "you can do it" generation. How often have you seen a pop star accepting an award and pouring out her mantra of "you can achieve your dream—just believe and keep following your heart," forgetting, of course, to let you know that for every award-winning, chart-topping superstar, there are tens of thousands of also-rans who never came anywhere near achieving such a dream.

The kingdom of God gives us a totally different idea of how to live the big life. Again and again, the Bible reminds us that the power of God in us is what will bring success in the kingdom of God:

> "Not by power, nor by might, but by my Spirit," says the LORD (Zech. 4:6).

> God chose the weak things of the world to shame the strong (1 Cor. 1:27).

> I delight in weaknesses. . . . For when I am weak, then I am strong (2 Cor. 12:10).

> But he said to me, "My grace is sufficient for you, for my power is made perfect in weakness." Therefore I will boast all the more gladly about my weaknesses, so that Christ's power may rest on me (2 Cor. 12:9).

The "you can do it" generation says, "I can do everything." But as women of God we complete the sentence: "I can do everything *through him who gives me strength*" (Phil. 4:13, emphasis added).

In the last few decades, society has taught women that strength and power must be fought for. Much of our culture has taught young females that there are only two ways to liberation and status—through aggression or seduction. The kingdom of God offers us a purer and more powerful way of being feminine and effective—Christ in our lives, the hope of glory. We surrender and He sustains us. We bow down and He empowers us.

We begin by acknowledging our own feebleness. Human willpower may get us through one or two days of the victorious life, but before long we'll be back on our knees where we first started. God has some beautiful ways of keeping us dependent on Him. And that's a very good thing. Take a look through the Bible and you'll notice the people of God have a dangerous habit of losing their dependence when things are on a roll. As my wise friend Darlene Zschech explained in the magazine *Worship Leader*:

> Momentum can be your best friend—it's like the breath of God, causing one day to be more valuable and worthwhile than a thousand. . . . But, you can abuse momentum if you stop digging for the gold that gave you that momentum in the first place. The very basics, the core values. Momentum can give you a false sense of security. "I'm awesome, we're awesome, we can do it!" But at what cost? Before we know it, we've abused the privilege and lost sight of the higher call.[1]

If we're to live a big life and be used powerfully in the kingdom of God, then reliance upon Him will always be the key. As Oswald Chambers so wisely wrote in the daily devotional *My Utmost for His Highest*, "Complete weakness and dependence will always be the occasion for the Spirit of God to manifest His power."[2]

I long to be part of a generation of young women who recognize their complete weakness but who realize God's complete strength. Women who pursue a godly life, along with faith, love, perseverance and gentleness. Who fight the good fight yet remain wholesomely feminine. A movement of young women who hold tightly to the things of God and the eternal life He has given them, yet hold lightly to the things of this world. Women who care for one another and sharpen one another, setting an example for others by living out their daily lives overflowing with love, joy, faith, purity, peace, patience, kindness, goodness, faithfulness, gentleness and self-control. A generation of women who live by the Spirit and keep in step with the Spirit.

If we're to live a big life and be used powerfully in the kingdom of God, then reliance upon Him will always be the key.

So do you want to be a beautiful woman of God? Here's the stunning, glorious key: Christ in you, the hope of glory!

Notes

1. Darlene Zschech, "The Power and Pitfalls of Success," Integrity Music. http://www.integritymusic.com/worship/zschech/1000.html (accessed January 2006).
2. Oswald Chambers, "Judgment on the Abyss of Love," *My Utmost for His Highest*, May 5th reading.

Mercy Ministries of America

Mercy Ministries of America is an international program for girls and young women between the ages of 13 and 28 who are dealing with eating disorders, chemical addictions, unplanned pregnancies, abuse and other life-controlling problems. The young women must voluntarily make an application to this free program. A willing heart and sincere desire to change are prerequisites for entering the program and beginning the ultimate path to transformation.

During their six- to eight-month stay, young women receive care from trained professionals at the residential facilities, completely free of charge. The daily schedule includes individual counseling, group counseling, life-skills training, food and fitness instruction, medical care, academic instruction, and other components for ensuring a productive future.

The ultimate goal of Mercy Ministries is that every young woman who completes the Mercy program will become a law-abiding, tax-paying individual who is self-supporting with independent-living skills, rather than depending on the government welfare system for support.

At Mercy, each young woman's restoration process is unique according to the severity of her problems, but the approach to her restoration is the same: to promote spiritual stability by demonstrating and teaching the unconditional love and mercy of God, combined with the practical application and training for daily life.

For more information on becoming a financial partner to Mercy Ministries, or if you or someone you know needs Mercy, please visit their website at www.mercyministries.com.

Other Books by
Beth Redman

Soul Sista
The Truth About Being God's Girl

Blessed Be Your Name
(Beth and Matt Redman)
Worshiping God on the Road Marked with Suffering

Soul Sister Series:

Soul Sister: Shine
Beautiful Inside and Out

Soul Sister: Connect
The Lowdown on Friends and Relationships

Soul Sister: Respect
How to Get It, How to Give It

More of the Best From
Beth Redman

BethRedman

This book is for soul sisters everywhere—a generation of girls living to please the heart of God.

There are lots of voices today telling us what to do and who to be. Some are subtle; some are obvious. Which ones should we trust?

The Bible speaks in a loud and clear voice into every area of life:

- The truth about identity
- The truth about forgiveness
- The truth about boys
- The truth about destiny

Beth Redman walks us through many of life's difficult issues and shows us how important it is to get into God's Word and to get God's Word into us.

Soul Sister • ISBN 08307.37316

Worship is always a choice. Come rain or shine, come hardship or ease, come confusion or clarity, the choice to worship God is a costly act of devotion. In the life of every worshipper there will come times when worship meets with suffering and the sovereignty of God. In *Blessed Be Your Name*, Matt and Beth Redman use the words of their inspiring song to explore how to stand in the place of praise even in the face of hardship and pain. Focusing on the Psalms, many of which were written out of struggle, the Redmans share from their own experience and show how painful circumstances and our choices can either propel us toward God or away from Him, build up our faith or break it. Learn how to ride out the storms of life with a cry of "blessed be Your name" on your lips.

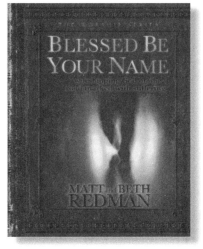

Blessed Be Your Name • ISBN 08307.38193

Inspiring Reading for Women

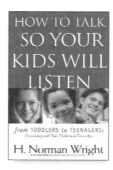

**Moments Together
for Couples**
Daily Devotions for Drawing Near
to God and One Another
Dennis and Barbara Rainey
ISBN 08307.17544

**Release the Pain,
Embrace the Joy**
Help for the Hurting Heart
Michelle McKinney Hammond
ISBN 08307.37227

**How to Talk So Your
Kids Will Listen**
From Toddlers to Teenagers—
Connecting with Your
Children at Every Age
H. Norman Wright
ISBN 08307.33280

Always Daddy's Girl
Understanding Your Father's
Impact on Who You Are
H. Norman Wright
ISBN 08307.27620

**Daily Steps for God
Chicks**
The 90 day devotional for
real women
Holly Wagner
ISBN 08307.39300

**The Measure of
a Woman**
What Really Makes a
Woman Beautiful
Gene A. Getz with Elaine Getz
ISBN 08307.32861